PURCHASING FROM SMALL MINORITY-OWNED FIRMS: CORPORATE PROBLEMS

by

Marc J. Dollinger

and

Catherine M. Daily

Center for Advanced Purchasing Studies
National Association of Purchasing Management

PURCHASING FROM SMALL MINORITY-OWNED FIRMS: CORPORATE PROBLEMS

by

Marc J. Dollinger, Ph.D.
and
Catherine M. Daily

School of Business
Department of Management
Indiana University

ACKNOWLEDGMENTS •

THE CENTER FOR ADVANCED PURCHASING STUDIES and the authors wish to thank the participants from 307 firms who provided the data on which this research report is based. We are also grateful for the project's major support from ARCO, Eli Lilly, Northern Telecom Inc., RJR Nabisco, Inc., and U S WEST.

We also thank Michelle Teague for her administrative and secretarial assistance; Richard Cosier, chairman of the Department of Management at Indiana University's School of Business, for his administrative support; and Jack Wentworth, dean of the School of Business at Indiana University, under whose auspices the study was completed in the Center for Entrepreneurship and Innovation.

At CAPS, thanks go to Carol Ketchum, administrative assistant; Richard Boyle, assistant director; Mary Ann Beckley, secretary; Laura Forker, graduate research associate; and Alan Campbell, graduate assistant; for editing and preparing the manuscript for publication.

Finally, six purchasing executives served on the ad-hoc industry/research/advisory committee. Their review of the manuscript helped strengthen its analysis and presentation. Special thanks are due to:

1. Kelvin Pillow, Northern Telecom Inc.
2. Bob Crowe, U S WEST Business Resources
3. Jerry Bathke, ARCO
4. Harold Jenkins, Nabisco Brands Inc.
5. Roger Oertel, Eli Lilly and Company
6. Sherry Embry, Bell Atlantic

Of course, complete responsibility for the final study rests with the authors of this report.

ISBN: 0-945968-03-5

LCCN: 89-60726

CONTENTS •

TABLES, EXHIBITS, AND APPENDICES •

PREFACE •

This report on the impediments facing small minority vendors and corporate purchasing managers from large firms seeks to give a broader understanding of those challenges. The report outlines the costs incurred by both sides when transactions between them are hampered by impediments; furthermore, it suggests some practical solutions to overcome these hindrances.

However, the report should not be taken as an all-inclusive statement about corporate purchasing from small minority-owned firms. Instead, it is hoped that this report encourages more research into the reasons why some barriers still exist and what may be done to remove them.

SUMMARY AND IMPLICATIONS OF THE STUDY •

The primary goal of corporate Minority Business Enterprise (MBE) purchasing programs is to enable small minority-owned firms to participate as vendors in the economic network of the corporation. Corporations have established these programs as a result of pressure from governmental and minority groups, of their own sense of social responsibility, and of the sound business practice of developing new vendors. There are, however, major impediments to successful transactions between large corporations and Minority Business Enterprises (MBEs) that participate in corporate MBE purchasing programs. This conclusion is based on a 1988 study sponsored by the National Association of Purchasing Management's Center for Advanced Purchasing Studies (CAPS). The major conclusions of the study are:

1. *MBEs participating in MBE purchasing programs face a series of higher transaction costs (the administrative costs of doing business) than do corporate purchasing personnel.* The MBEs' most severe problems are in the areas of: dealing with the complex, bureaucratic nature of large purchasing units; maintaining quality performance; insuring the survival of their businesses; eliminating the potential for opportunistic and unethical behavior; receiving and sending information about their firms; and dealing in a sometimes hostile and unfriendly environment.

2. *MBEs favor activities designed to overcome these transaction costs more than their corporate purchasing counterparts do.* These activities take the following forms: (a) activities designed to improve the internal monitoring of MBE purchasing programs; (b) activities designed to improve the "search" procedure for both MBEs and purchasing personnel by making it easier for each side to find the other; (c) the provision of financial, managerial, and technical assistance to MBEs; (d) increased opportunities for personal interaction between individuals of different cultural backgrounds; and (e) activities that bring the MBE closer to the corporation, within the usual "arms-length" contractual mode.

3. *MBEs more strongly favor programs with multiple criteria for evaluation.* Both MBEs and purchasing personnel agree that increasing buyer portfolios of MBE suppliers and using MBE vendors creatively are the best criteria for evaluation. Both sides also agree that fulfilling federal quotas is the least desirable criterion.

4. *In certain instances the respondent's race was more important in how some questions were answered than whether the person was from an MBE, a large corporation, or a non-minority small business.*

5. *There are as many differences between MBEs and SBEs (small business enterprises, non-minority-owned) as between MBEs and corporate purchasing personnel (CPPs).* This indicates that MBEs and SBEs do not face the same set of circumstances and transaction costs when selling to large corporations. Some of these differences are attributable to the larger size of the non-minority firms and some apparently to their non-minority status.

6. *There are few important differences between corporate respondents from the eight industries represented in the study.* While some idiosyncratic differences arise, the impediments are not inherent in any particular industry in a systematic way.

7. *There are important differences between corporate respondents with different job titles on the activities recommended to overcome the impediments to MBE purchasing programs.* Buyers and purchasing agents are less enthusiastic about most activities than are their managers, corporate staff personnel, or corporate executives—because buyers probably have to implement these activities, thereby raising the personal transaction costs of their jobs.

8. *The minority respondents report higher levels of graduate-degree completion than do either the corporate purchasing personnel or the non-minority small business owner.* This finding suggests that well-educated minorities find career paths in large firms blocked and that they choose entrepreneurship as an avenue for advancement.

9. *The average corporate buyer has a much shorter tenure on the job than does the MBE.* Rapid turnover among corporate purchasing agents may contribute to the problems MBEs face.

INTRODUCTION •

The potential social and economic consequences of minority entrepreneurship are immense. The development of a strong and independent minority business sector has been recognized as a major societal priority by the government, the corporate business community, and the minority community. To promote minority entrepreneurship, programs have been established to give the minority business enterprises access to the mainstream of business opportunity.

All corporations that do business with the federal government are required to contract with and purchase from small and minority business enterprises (MBEs). Public Law 95-507 of 1978 requires contractors to submit subcontract plans for approval and to report their progress in achieving a specific percentage of business with small minority firms. Public Law 99-661 of 1986 requires Department of Defense contractors to make 5 percent of their purchases from small minority businesses, including businesses owned and operated by blacks, Hispanics, Asians of Pacific origin, and native Americans. [1] Additionally, hundreds of corporations that have no federal mandate pursue minority suppliers and vendors to increase opportunities for MBEs, in order to meet professional standards for ethical purchasing, to generate minority employment, and to fulfill their social responsibility. For many businesses, however, complying with legal requirements and attaining corporate MBE objectives present an apparently intractable problem. Attempts to meet these requirements and voluntary efforts to aid in the economic development of minority and small businesses often end in failure and frustration for both parties.

This study focuses on the impediments and problems that large corporations have in purchasing from MBEs and smaller companies. *It looks at the problems of MBE purchasing programs from both the corporate buyer's and MBE vendor's viewpoints.* The theoretical framework for the study is based on transaction costs and the theory of transaction cost economics (TCE). TCE theory enables us to identify the sources of transaction costs. Interactions between economic units can be analyzed based upon the nature and outcomes of individual transactions and the costs of executing these transactions. This analysis applies to the scenario of a minority business enterprise selling a product or service to a large corporation. TCE theory would predict that if transactions between an MBE vendor and corporate buyer are difficult to execute, then the costs of the transaction are high for both the corporation and the minority firm. According to the theory, under these conditions the parties would choose internal administration as the most efficient alternative. However, the option of internal governance is not available here. In order to meet federal guidelines and social objectives, the parties must remain legally distinct and the MBE independent.

When TCE is applied to the problems of MBE purchasing programs, the important issue becomes the different transaction cost constraints faced by the corporation and the MBE. If the gap between the MBE and the purchasing corporation is too large, the parties will be unable to agree on solutions. This study looks at these transaction costs and suggests solutions within the TCE framework. Data from field interviews and a large sample field survey are employed to test for differences between MBE vendors and CPPs.

---

[1] These designations are the ones that appear in federal guidelines.

DESIGN OF THE STUDY •

STUDY GOALS

This study was sponsored by the Center for Advanced Purchasing Studies (CAPS). The primary objectives of this research were:

1. To determine the impediments to minority business enterprise (MBE) purchasing programs.

2. To survey the extent to which MBEs and corporate purchasing personnel (CPPs) differed on these impediments.

3. To examine the extent to which these impediments were a function of the size of the firm or the racial and cultural backgrounds of the MBEs.

4. To determine which activities to overcome the impediments were preferred by MBEs and which were preferred by corporate purchasing personnel (CPPs).

5. To examine MBE and CPP preferences for criteria in evaluating the success or failure of MBE purchasing programs.

6. To determine the importance of business values and business value similarity in the process of MBE purchasing.

PHASES OF THE STUDY

The study was conducted in four distinct phases. The first phase assessed the current knowledge and practice in the area of minority business enterprise by reviewing literature and previous studies (see Appendix A) and by conducting a series of interviews with corporate purchasing personnel and minority business people. (See Appendix B.) The second phase involved the development of a questionnaire, the recruitment of corporate and minority firms, and the execution of the study. (See Appendix C.) The third phase was data analysis. The questions on the survey were recombined into scales that represent the variables in the transaction cost economics (TCE) framework. (See Appendix D, which describes the method for constructing the scales and shows which questions from the survey make up the variables.)

THE SAMPLE •

DATA

Interviews were conducted in the spring of 1988. Ten MBE firms as well as purchasing personnel from 13 corporations were interviewed. Corporate participants were selected at random from the National Association of Purchasing Management's membership list. Minority participants were selected from the *Try Us '88 Directory of Minority Business.* The interviews were conducted at the subjects' place of business. An interview schedule was designed and used by the interviewers; however, many questions were open-ended and intended to elicit the experiences of the individuals. (See Appendix B for interview results.)

Based upon an analysis of the interview data, a survey instrument was designed and pretested. (See Appendix C for the survey instrument and cover letters.) A three-part field study was then conducted. MBEs were again surveyed at random from the *Try Us '88 Directory of Minority Business.* Four hundred seventy-five surveys were sent; 169 usable responses were received (two mailings) for a response rate of 35.6 percent. The MBEs surveyed represented 83 different 4-digit SIC codes and 112 different 3-digit ZIP codes. Table 1 summarizes the response rates and degree of participation in the study for all three groups: minority firms (MBEs), small businesses (SBEs), and corporations (CPPs).

A group of small businesses (SBEs) was selected at random from Harris's *Industrial Directory of Indiana* (1988) and sent the identical survey except for the substitution of the abbreviation SBE for MBE in each item. This group of small firms is not the ideal control group because of its limited geographic coverage and its focus on manufacturing firms. However, time and budget considerations intervened.

Four hundred eighty surveys were sent (two mailings) and 115 usable responses were received for a response rate of 24 percent. (See Table 1.) The response rate for SBEs was lower than that for MBEs because the questionnaire did not have the same importance for the SBEs. This difference exists because fewer non-minority SBEs participate in specially designed SBE purchasing programs. Overall, SBEs are less familiar with the issues of purchasing programs. SBEs responded from 69 different 4-digit SIC codes and 11 different 3-digit ZIP codes. The SBEs were included as a control group to examine the effects caused by the size of a firm. If the analysis showed that the MBEs and the SBEs viewed the problems in the same way, then it could be concluded that the problems, or impediments, could be attributed to a firm's small size. If, on the other hand, differences emerged between MBEs and SBEs on the impediments, these differences would be due to race and culture.

Table 2 shows that there were no statistical differences between respondents (R) and non-respondents (NR) based upon the firm's sales and the number of employees, for the SBE (t=1.50, 1.14) and MBE (t=.24, .33) groups.

TABLE 1
RESPONSE RATES AND PARTICIPATION

Group	Mailing #1	Mailing #2	Other	Total	Response Rate
Minority Firms (MBE)	112	54	3	169	35.6%
Small Businesses (SBE)	61	52	2	115	24.0%

	First Contacts	Second Contacts	Response Rate
Corporations (CPP) (23 Firms) (n=746)	12/20 (60%)	11/63 (17.5%)	27.7%

	Number of 4-Digit SICs	Number of 3-Digit ZIPs	Divisions
Minority Firms	83	112	N/A
Small Businesses	69	11	N/A
Corporations	21(8 2-digit)	102	103

TABLE 2
RESPONDENTS (R) VERSUS NON-RESPONDENTS (NR)

Group	Sales ($1,000) R	Sales ($1,000) NR	Employees (Number) R	Employees (Number) NR	t Value Sales	t Value Employees
SBE (stan'd deviation)	7,572 (24,196)	2,281 (5,623)	44.0 (42.2)	49.5 (50.4)	1.50	1.14
MBE (stan'd deviation)	2,430 (4,054)	2,325 (3,926)	33.3 (75.1)	31.1 (61.1)	.24	.33

The SBE firms were, however, larger than the MBE firms in sales (not statistically significant) and number of employees (t=5.13, p<.001). The purpose of including the SBEs in the study was to isolate the impediments owing to size from those owing to race or culture. Although the SBEs are larger than the MBEs, they are still predominantly white-owned and very much smaller than the large corporations. Table 3 displays these differences.

TABLE 3
SBEs VERSUS MBEs

Variable	SBE	MBE	t value
Sales ($1,000)	4,324	2,345	1.62
(standard deviation)	(15,502)	(3,907)	
Employees	50.2	31.1	5.13**
(standard deviation)	(50.4)	(64.7)	
Age of Respondent	48.0	45.3	1.98*
(standard deviation)	(11.2)	(9.9)	
Number of Years in Current Position	13.2	10.8	2.07*
(standard deviation)	(10.9)	(6.4)	

* Indicates statistical significance at the 0.05 level
** Indicates statistical significance at the 0.001 level

The third group sampled consisted of corporate purchasing personnel (CPPs). Out of 83 firms approached from the membership of the National Minority Supplier Development Association, 23 firms agreed to participate (27.7 percent). From these 23 firms, 746 usable surveys were returned from purchasing agents (buyers), their managers, corporate staff involved in MBE purchasing programs, and corporate executives with MBE responsibility. The average number of responses returned by each firm was slightly over 34, with the high at 119 and the low at 4. The corporate respondents represented 103 corporate divisions, 102 separate 3-digit ZIP codes, 21 4-digit SIC codes, and 8 different 2-digit SIC codes. The geographically dispersed nature of the sample coupled with the diversity of businesses represented increases the generalizability of the results.

Additional information concerning the characteristics of all respondents is presented in Table 4.

TABLE 4
CHARACTERISTICS OF THE RESPONDENTS

	MBE (n=169)		SBE (n=115)		CPP (n=746)	
	#	%	#	%	#	%
Race:						
Caucausian	9	(5.3)	100	(87.0)	639	(85.7)
Black	75	(44.4)	4	(4.0)	53	(7.1)
Hispanic	45	(26.6)	0	(0.0)	9	(1.2)
Asian-American	31	(18.3)	2	(1.7)	11	(1.5)
Native American	7	(4.1)	9	(7.8)	16	(2.1)
Other/Not Stated	2	(1.2)	0	(0.0)	18	(2.4)
Sex:						
Male	124	(73.4)	94	(81.7)	509	(68.2)
Female	42	(24.9)	20	(17.4)	225	(30.2)
Not Stated	3	(1.8)	1	(0.9)	12	(1.6)
Education:						
Less than High School	2	(1.2)	3	(2.6)	1	(0.1)
High School Graduate	15	(8.9)	16	(13.9)	42	(5.6)
Some College	41	(24.3)	31	(27.0)	169	(22.7)
College Graduate	38	(22.5)	38	(33.0)	279	(37.4)
Some Graduate School	26	(15.4)	9	(7.8)	127	(17.0)
Graduate Degree	45	(26.6)	17	(14.8)	116	(15.5)
Not Stated	2	(1.2)	1	(0.9)	12	(1.6)
Origin of Birth:						
Large City	78	(46.2)	47	(40.9)	323	(43.3)
Small City	42	(24.9)	42	(36.5)	249	(33.4)
Rural Area	45	(26.6)	25	(21.7)	165	(22.1)
Not Stated	4	(2.4)	1	(0.9)	9	(1.2)
Age (avg.):	45.3		48.0		42.2	
Number of Years on Job (avg.):	10.8		13.2		6.1	

	#	%	#	%		
Title (MBE/SBE):						
Owner	126	(74.6)	75	(65.2)		
Senior Manager	23	(13.6)	25	(21.7)		
Junior Manager	4	(2.4)	1	(0.9)		
Not Stated	16	(9.5)	14	(12.2)		

	#	%
Title (CPP):		
Buyer	371	(49.7)
Manager	170	(22.8)
Corporate Staff	54	(7.2)
Corporate Executive	10	(1.3)
Not Stated	141	(18.9)

Table 4 profiles the characteristics of each of the three groups in the study. The major variables are: race, sex, education, origin of birth, average age, average years on the job, and title. These characteristics were collected on Page 4 of the survey. (See Appendix C.)

As expected, the MBE sample is overwhelmingly non-white (94.7 percent). The nine respondents in the MBE sample who identified themselves as white may represent a cultural minority such as Hispanic, or may be white non-owners (employees) of the firm. There is no evidence to indicate that these are really non-minority firms. On the other hand, the SBE and CPP samples are overwhelmingly white.

Blacks represent only 4 percent of the SBE sample and 7.1 percent of the CPP sample.

The majority of respondents in all three samples are male. The lowest percentage of women are in the SBE group (17.4 percent), followed by the MBE group (24.9 percent). The corporate group has the largest percentage of women represented (30.2 percent). There was no statistical difference in responses based on sex.

The next variable reported in Table 4 is education. Because the survey form was relatively long and fairly complicated, it is possible that individuals with little formal education are underrepresented in the sample. Well over half the respondents from each group had completed college, and 26.6 percent of the MBE respondents had graduate degrees, versus 14.8 percent of the SBEs and 15.5 percent of the CPPs. The high percentage of minority respondents with graduate degrees suggest that minorities who might otherwise be productively employed in large corporations have found an alternative in entrepreneurship. This may be because corporate career opportunities were blocked, or perhaps entrepreneurial opportunities were too rewarding to pass up. In any case, minority entrepreneurs are a well-educated group.

There are few differences in "Origin of Birth" for the respondents, with most having been born in a large city. There were no differences in responses to the other questions based on origin of birth. Also, SBE respondents were the oldest, averaging 48 years old, while MBEs and CPPs averaged 45.3 and 42.2, respectively.

There is a large and statistically significant (F=19.70, p<.001) difference between the MBE/SBE sample and the CPPs for the number of years on the job, which indicates the rapid turnover in corporate purchasing personnel. The ownership of a small, established business is apparently a more stable endeavor. Although this finding was not specifically investigated in the survey, it may have major consequences for the corporate and minority business relationship. Corporate purchasing personnel often have a great degree of authority to negotiate and award contracts. This authority makes the personal relationship between vendor and procurement officer important. But when a reliable minority vendor faces a new purchasing agent, that vendor may have to re-prove his/her firm's reliability. The memory of the corporation is always being wiped clean by turnover and internal job switching.

Over 88 percent of the MBE sample is composed of owners or senior managers. The percentage for the SBE sample is 86.9 percent. Therefore, the

people who were in the best position to know their firm's experience with corporate purchasing programs were the people who filled out the questionnaires. Almost half the corporate respondents identified themselves as buyers (49.7 percent), while 22.8 percent identified themselves as managers of buyers. Thus, almost 75 percent of the CPP sample is in a position that has direct-line responsibility for executing MBE purchasing programs. The large number of Other/Not Stated data for this variable may be due to the question's position on the survey (at the bottom of the last page). This code will not be used in the examination of the effects of job title on impediments, which appears later in the study.

The purpose of this section has been to establish the external and representative validity of the sample. This has been done by showing that there were no differences (in a statistical sense) between those individuals that returned the survey and those that did not. In addition, it was shown that the MBE and CPP surveys were returned by individuals from all over the country, from many different types of businesses. Lastly, the respondents were grouped in a valid manner, that is, the MBEs were overwhelmingly minority individuals, the SBEs predominantly non-minority, and the CPPs directly involved in MBE purchasing programs as buyers and managers. Therefore, it can be concluded that the data collected in this study represent a valid cross section of opinion and experience in MBE purchasing programs.

THE VARIABLES

Variables were created out of the items in the survey to represent the dimensions of the transaction costs framework. The theoretical derivations of these variables are described in Appendix A. Exhibit 1 presents brief definitions of these variables.

EXHIBIT 1

**SUMMARY DESCRIPTIONS OF THE
IMPEDIMENT VARIABLES IN THE STUDY**

Small Numbers: The costs of attempting to contract for goods and services in a market with a small number of sellers.

Complexity: The costs of dealing with complex rules, large bureaucracies, and inconsistent procedures.

Business Uncertainty: The costs of maintaining the firm's prospects for performance and survival.

Production Uncertainty: The costs of achieving, maintaining, and insuring high-quality output.

Opportunism: The costs associated with opportunistic, unethical, or illegal behavior.

Impacted Information: The costs of obtaining information that one side to a negotiation has available but the other does not.

Atmosphere: The personal costs of doing business in a hostile, unfriendly atmosphere.

Resource Dependence: The extent to which one party in a contractual negotiation depends on the contract for vital resources. This is a measure of power.

Value Similarity: The degree of value sharing.

Value Importance: The level of value importance.

Appendix D details the mechanics of variable construction and lists the individual items that make up the variables. Table 5 displays the means, standard deviations, and other information for the impediments variables. The last column, "Alpha," shows a measure of the reliability (or internal consistency) of the scale. Only the variable "Opportunism" falls below an acceptable standard of .70 for this type of field research.

TABLE 5

**IMPEDIMENT SCALE MEANS,
STANDARD DEVIATIONS, AND RELIABILITIES**

Variable Name	Mean	Standard Deviation	Item Mean	Number of Items	Alpha
Small Numbers	33.92	7.51	4.24	8	.70
Complexity	66.03	15.89	3.88	17	.85
Business Uncertainty	16.99	5.14	4.25	4	.79
Production Uncertainty	18.71	5.20	3.74	5	.71
Opportunism	16.91	4.95	4.23	4	.62
Impacted Information	27.94	7.95	3.99	7	.77
Atmosphere	20.53	6.24	4.10	5	.75
Resource Dependence	47.31	10.63	3.94	12	.76
Value Similarity	79.40	12.18	3.97	20	.90
Value Importance	84.89	7.86	4.24	20	.82

Table 6 shows the same information for the "Activity" variables. Again, there are a few variables that have low reliabilities: searching for MBEs, providing managerial assistance, and encouraging cultural interaction. Because these variables are constructed from items that represent different activities, the above statement is not surprising.

However, some caution should be used in interpreting the results for these variables.

TABLE 6

**ACTIVITY SCALE MEANS,
STANDARD DEVIATIONS, AND RELIABILITIES**

Scale Name	Mean	Standard Deviation	Item Mean	Number of Items	Alpha
Monitoring of MBEs	32.16	5.08	5.35	6	.71
Monitoring of CPPs	55.91	11.23	5.08	11	.87
Searching for MBEs	31.30	5.51	5.21	6	.64
Searching for CPPs	32.33	6.36	5.39	6	.81
Financial Assistance	10.37	4.57	3.46	3	.78
Managerial Assistance	21.21	4.01	5.30	4	.56
Technical Assistance	12.73	4.26	4.24	3	.74
Cultural Interaction	15.43	3.41	5.14	3	.64
Internalization	17.38	5.27	4.34	4	.78

To summarize this section concerning the reliability of the variables, 10 variables were constructed to represent "Impediments," and nine variables were constructed to represent groups of "Activities" that could overcome these impediments. Overall, the variables displayed acceptable degrees of reliability for this type of research. Both the external validity demonstrated in the previous section and the internal consistency of the variables are necessary to interpret the results.

PURCHASING FROM SMALL MINORITY-OWNED FIRMS: CORPORATE PROBLEMS •

The results are presented in three parts. The first part analyzes the impediments, activities, and criteria for evaluation for differences by group (MBE, SBE, and CPP) and race. The second section presents a similar analysis for differences by industry. The third section reports differences within the corporate sample by job title. Before reporting these three sections, the three sets of variables are presented in rank order for the combined sample.

Figure 1 reports the rank order of importance for the impediment variables for the total sample. Figure 2 reports the rank order of importance for the activities, and Figure 3 reports the ranks of the criteria for evaluation. Appendix E contains tables that report the rank orders for the items in the questionnaire for each of the three groups in the sample and for the combined sample. These tables, E1 through E20, report the top 15 and bottom 15 items.

FIGURE 1

RANK ORDER OF IMPEDIMENT SCALES
(On a Scale of 1 to 7)

Rank	Variable	Mean
1	Business Uncertainty	4.25
2	Small Numbers	4.24
3	Opportunism	4.23
4	Atmosphere	4.10
5	Impacted Information	3.99
6	Resource Dependence	3.94
7	Complexity	3.88
8	Prod. Uncertainty	3.74

Figure 1 indicates that the primary problem for the combined sample is the transaction cost of business uncertainty. Close behind it are the problems of small numbers and opportunism. Atmosphere is the fourth-ranked problem. Because the respondents were asked to rank items on a seven-point scale (see Appendix C), scores between 4 and 5 represent slight agreement and scores between 3 and 4 slight disagreement. Therefore, for the combined sample, only the top four impediments were rated as problems, and people slightly disagreed overall that the bottom four impediments were problems.

Figure 2 shows the rank orders for the activity variables for the combined sample.

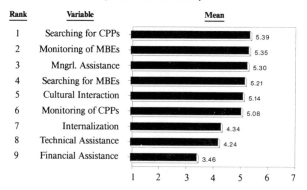

FIGURE 2

RANK ORDER OF ACTIVITY SCALES
(On a Scale of 1 to 7)

Rank	Variable	Mean
1	Searching for CPPs	5.39
2	Monitoring of MBEs	5.35
3	Mngrl. Assistance	5.30
4	Searching for MBEs	5.21
5	Cultural Interaction	5.14
6	Monitoring of CPPs	5.08
7	Internalization	4.34
8	Technical Assistance	4.24
9	Financial Assistance	3.46

Figure 2 shows that the primary recommended activity is searching for CPPs, which means making it easier for MBEs to find and participate in corporate purchasing programs. Numbers 2 through 6 respectively are: monitoring MBE performance; offering MBEs managerial assistance; making it easier for corporations to search for MBEs; improving cultural interaction; and developing the capability to monitor internal corporate implementation of MBE purchasing programs. Each of these activities is rated above a 5.0 and is therefore between slightly agree and moderately agree. There is slight positive agreement on the value of internalization and technical assistance, and slight disagreement on the value of financial assistance.

Figure 3 shows the rank order for the criteria for evaluating MBE purchasing programs.

FIGURE 3

CRITERIA FOR EVALUATING MBE PURCHASING PROGRAMS
(On a Scale of 1 to 7)

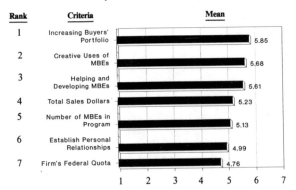

Rank	Criteria	Mean
1	Increasing Buyers' Portfolio	5.85
2	Creative Uses of MBEs	5.68
3	Helping and Developing MBEs	5.61
4	Total Sales Dollars	5.23
5	Number of MBEs in Program	5.13
6	Establish Personal Relationships	4.99
7	Firm's Federal Quota	4.76

All seven methods of evaluating MBE purchasing programs received support. The top-ranked criteria were: increasing buyers' portfolio, creative uses of MBEs, and helping and developing MBEs. These all received moderately high agreement. Further down were total sales dollars and number of MBEs in the program, which are traditionally popular criteria for evaluation. There was slight agreement on establishing personal relationships and meeting the firm's federal quota.

ANALYSIS OF IMPEDIMENTS BY GROUP, RACE, AND EDUCATION

Figure 4 shows how the different groups responded on the impediments variables. The variable means are shown. A complete one-way analysis of variance, including a display of statistical significance, is presented in Table F1 in Appendix F. (Values are not comparable between impediment categories because of uneven scale lengths.)

FIGURE 4

SUMMARY OF IMPEDIMENTS BY GROUP

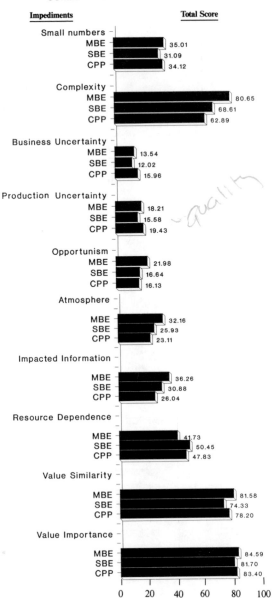

Figure 4 shows that there are important differences on practically all the impediments. In fact, all the differences between MBEs and CPPs are statistically significant except for those concerning small numbers and value importance. (See Table F1, Appendix F.) All the differences between the MBEs and the SBEs, except for those concerning business uncertainty and value importance, are also statistically significant.

Figure 4 tells us that both the minority-owned firms and the corporate purchasing personnel are acutely aware of the problems caused by the small number of MBEs available within the economy. While the problem for the CPPs is clearly one of scarcity and the extra expense of finding MBEs, the problem is different for the minority firms on the other side of the equation. The "small numbers" problem for MBEs means that the minority business community, in many areas of the country, has not reached the critical mass needed for legitimacy. The members of the MBE community don't have the networks and connections they need to act as references for each other. Often, they cannot even buy from each other because there is a shortage of reliable suppliers *within* the MBE community. One very successful East Coast minority-owned firm reported that they were disappointed in their search for MBE vendors—there weren't enough to be a plausible alternative. The problem called small numbers is rated lowest by the SBEs, reflecting the omnipresence of small business enterprises.

A major difference exists between MBEs and the CPPs on the dimension of complexity. The large organization confronts the MBE with its bureaucracy and all its rules, procedures, policies, and programs. The CPP must manage the complexity of the purchasing area for one organization. However, the MBE owner must manage this complexity for each organization he/she sells to *and* manage the entire MBE organization. This makes the MBE's task much more complex than the CPP's. It is no wonder that MBEs report problems of intimidating bureaucracy. Here the burden is unbalanced, with the weight more heavily borne by the MBEs.

Another major difference between MBEs and CPPs is found in the impediment called business uncertainty, which refers to the problems of operating the MBE business and insuring its survival. The CPPs are more skeptical about the abilities of the MBEs. This variable is one of only two in which the MBEs and SBEs are in agreement; apparently, the owners of the smaller firms are more confident about their firms' business performance than are the CPPs. It is possible that, to the CPP living in the relatively well-ordered world of the corporation, the smaller firms appear chaotic and always on the verge of a crisis. From the vantage point of the small business owner, this chaos is quite familiar and part of being an entrepreneur.

Production uncertainty, the quality issue, is most worrisome to the CPPs, then to the MBEs, followed by the SBEs. This is not surprising because the buyer is often more concerned and skeptical about the quality of the product than is the seller. The cost of poor quality and the cost of monitoring production to control quality are incurred by the MBE and the CPP. Although the difference is small between the two groups, it is statistically significant. During the interviews, CPPs were always able to recall an incident in which an MBE's quality was poor and the order needed extensive rework or was rejected. Interestingly, the MBEs could usually point to another MBE for an example of poor quality. The MBE is sensitive to poor quality because it reinforces the stereotype of minority business as incompetent and hurts the reputation of all competent MBEs. As one MBE consultant put it, there are three kinds of MBE firms: qualified, qualifiable, and unqualified. The majority of firms are qualifiable or unqualified, and telling them apart is difficult at first glance. But the unqualified vendor spoils the field for the others.

Opportunism is seen as a larger impediment by the MBEs than by either corporate purchasing personnel or the SBEs. Opportunism reflects both the issues of "minority-front" organizations and unethical behavior on the part of the purchasing people. On this issue, it is the MBEs who are skeptical about the performance of their CPP counterparts. Buyers who manipulate MBEs to achieve internal goals, who play office politics, or who simply lack commitment represent a cost to the MBE. While the MBE is expending scarce resources of time, energy, and money to win a corporate contract, he/she has no possible chance to win that contract. While the extent to which the problem exists was not measured in this study, the impact of this impediment exists both perceptually and "out-of-pocket" for the MBE.

The atmosphere impediment refers to the potential for cultural and racial bias. Individuals who find it unpleasant to deal with each other also find it costly to negotiate. This problem is seen as significantly larger by the MBEs than by the corporate personnel, with the non-minority SBEs again in an intermediate position but closer to the CPPs. Clearly, the MBEs bear the burden of racial and cultural prejudice. CPPs admit privately that they know of others who are prejudiced and don't like to deal with "them." MBEs can often point to examples of discrimination against themselves, friends, or business acquaintances. One MBE rationalized it this way: A non-minority CPP may not feel that he/she is prejudiced, but discrimination in society is strong. Poor quality and irregular business practices occur in many small businesses, but when they happen in an MBE, they are attributed to race instead of misjudgment.

Impacted information, the inability to receive information that is material without incurring a cost, also represents a major difference between the groups. CPPs see this problem as less severe than the minorities do, with SBEs in the intermediate position. As MBEs see it, the information they receive from the corporation is often difficult to understand, incomplete, or too late. MBEs report a common problem of receiving an offer to bid just days before a deadline. However, the problem has another side. MBEs are often fearful that they will not receive business if the buyer finds out that the MBE is having business or production difficulties. Even an open-minded CPP cannot alleviate a problem if he/she doesn't know about it. MBEs are extremely reluctant to share any sort of negative information. Clearly, this problem derives from some of the problems mentioned above: uncertainty, opportunism, and atmosphere.

The last three variables in Figure 4 are not related to transaction cost but are included in the study as alternative explanations. Resource dependence is a measure of power. MBEs score themselves quite low on this dimension. They see themselves as being dependent on others for their business resources. This dependence is in stark contrast to non-minority SBEs who view themselves as being powerful and autonomous. The corporate personnel consider the MBEs to be as powerful as the SBEs. The exact source of the MBEs' sense of powerlessness and dependence is not known, but it may come from the high cost of securing resources, transacting business, and, psychologically, dealing with an apparently hostile environment. An alternative explanation is that the powerlessness is fostered by programs that increase dependence, albeit unintentionally, as do MBE purchasing programs.

Although the three groups show no differences on the variable of value importance, they show statistically significant differences on the variable of value similarity. The MBEs report that they thought their values were similar to those held by top corporate management. Neither the SBEs nor the corporate personnel thought their values were similar to those of the MBEs. This seems to suggest that the MBE owners have a stronger desire to fit in and share the values of corporate America than do either of the other two groups. Apparently, the MBEs are very motivated to see the large corporation's viewpoint.

Table F2 (see Appendix F) reports the extent to which differences arise from the respondent's group, race, or education.

The results of this analysis are summarized as follows: The respondent's race significantly affects the variables of business uncertainty, complexity, opportunism, impacted information, atmosphere, and resource dependence. This indicates that, independent of which group the individual was in, the individual's racial/cultural identity affected the way the questions were answered. Nonwhites and other minorities consistently agreed that the above impediments were more important to them than to whites. The effect of education approached significance only for the atmosphere variable. This suggests that better-educated respondents were more sensitive to the bias issue and more likely to recognize it when it occurred.

Figure 5 presents the results for the three groups on the activity variables. The MBE responses differ from the CPP responses on all the variables except on the monitoring of MBEs. Without exception, the MBEs favor the implementation of these activities more than do the SBEs or the CPPs. MBEs also differ from SBEs on all scales except monitoring and technical assistance. SBE responses differ from CPP responses on all scales except the desire for cultural interaction and searching for SBEs, which suggests the influence of size and race. The complete one-way analysis of variance for these results is presented in Appendix F as Table F3.

FIGURE 5

SUMMARY OF RECOMMENDED ACTIVITIES BY GROUP

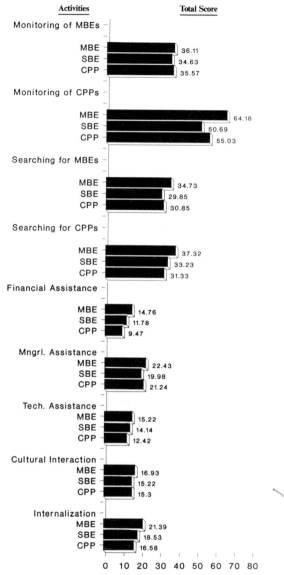

Activities · Total Score

Monitoring of MBEs
- MBE 36.11
- SBE 34.63
- CPP 35.57

Monitoring of CPPs
- MBE 64.18
- SBE 50.69
- CPP 55.03

Searching for MBEs
- MBE 34.73
- SBE 29.85
- CPP 30.85

Searching for CPPs
- MBE 37.32
- SBE 33.23
- CPP 31.33

Financial Assistance
- MBE 14.76
- SBE 11.78
- CPP 9.47

Mngrl. Assistance
- MBE 22.43
- SBE 19.98
- CPP 21.24

Tech. Assistance
- MBE 15.22
- SBE 14.14
- CPP 12.42

Cultural Interaction
- MBE 16.93
- SBE 15.22
- CPP 15.3

Internalization
- MBE 21.39
- SBE 18.53
- CPP 16.58

0 10 20 30 40 50 60 70 80

Not surprisingly, MBEs strongly favor activities that promote MBE purchasing, because they are the major beneficiaries. Also, each of these activities can be linked to the transaction costs that they are intended to lower. For example, monitoring activities can reduce uncertainty and the threat of opportunism. Searching activities help lower the costs of small numbers and impacted information. Various kinds of assistance reduce complexity and improve performance reliability. Cultural interaction reduces bias and improves the atmosphere within which negotiations take place. The final category of activity, internalization, addresses all these issues by bringing the MBE and the corporation closer than the tradi-

tional arms-length contracting position. Internalization has the potential to be the most powerful of all the activities, because the closer the MBE to the corporation, the lower their transaction costs. Therefore, exchange between the MBE and the CPP can be made more easily.

An example of this type of closeness emerged from many interviews, from both the MBEs and CPPs. It seems that some of the most successful MBE/corporate relationships that people can recall are those in which a former minority employee leaves the corporation and goes into business for himself/herself. In this case, a previously internalized transaction (an employment contract) is transformed into a market transaction (a contractor). Yet many of the characteristics of the internal form remain.

The newly external MBE entrepreneur knows the system of his/her former corporation, and this reduces complexity a great deal. Because the former employee's skill, ability, and motivation are well-known by his/her former employers, uncertainty is also reduced to a minimum. Although the overall problem of small numbers is not significantly changed, at least one more legitimate MBE is available. Opportunism is sharply reduced because neither the MBE nor his/her former colleagues would take advantage of the situation. Information is freely disseminated because each party already knows most of the necessary facts. Lastly, the atmosphere problem is greatly reduced: Although bias and prejudice may exist for the MBE population at large, the former employee is treated as a family member, a "good" minority person.

To summarize the results of the activities that reduce impediments, MBEs consistently recommend these activities more strongly than do CPPs. These activities help reduce transaction costs. Activities that partly or totally internalize the MBE firm may be the most effective method of reducing transaction costs.

A more in-depth analysis was conducted to determine the effects of different activities recommended because of race/culture identity. (See Table F4 in Appendix F.)

These results can be summarized as follows: In addition to the effects by group as previously reported in Figure 5, Table F4 in Appendix F illustrates the importance of race/culture identity. All the activities had significant effects for race/culture orientation. In searching for MBEs, managerial assistance, and cultural interaction, the effect of race is greater than that of group. These results indicate that nonwhites and minorities look more favorably

17

on these activities than do whites and non-minorities, regardless of which of the three groups the respondents belong to.

Figure 6 displays the results by group for the criteria for evaluating MBE purchasing programs. Table F5 presents the one-way analysis of variance and identifies statistically significant differences. (See Appendix F.)

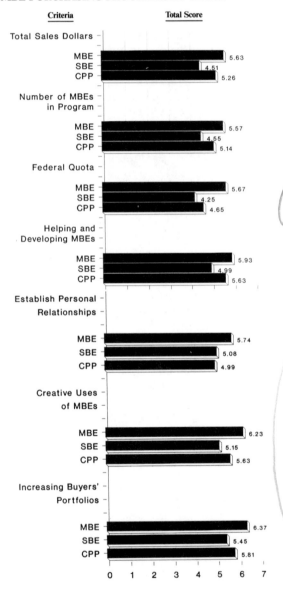

FIGURE 6

SUMMARY OF CRITERIA FOR EVALUATING
MBE PURCHASING PROGRAMS BY GROUP

The MBEs felt more strongly about these seven evaluation criteria than did either the SBEs or the corporate purchasing personnel. There was a sta-

tistical difference between MBEs and SBEs on all items and a difference between MBEs and corporate personnel on all items except total sales dollars and developing MBE vendors. (See Appendix F, Table F5.)

These results seem to indicate that multiple criteria are needed to evaluate MBE purchasing programs. Because the programs themselves are multi-dimensional, more than a single dimension is needed to evaluate success or failure. The MBEs recognize that evaluation criteria are often linked to incentives; therefore, MBEs favor all possible criteria and incentives more strongly than do the CPPs.

The corporate personnel recognize this link, too, and seem to prefer criteria that are somewhat vaguer (creative uses and increased portfolios). Among the least respected criteria are the federal quota and total sales dollars. During interviews for this research, a number of CPPs and MBEs addressed these two criteria. They reported that the federal quota was usually not enforced and that there seldom were audits to check for compliance. Without that monitoring, a cynicism about the federal quota has developed. And the criterion of total sales dollars is also suspect. CPPs report that, because many MBEs are clustered in the same low-tech industries, they compete mostly against each other. There is a limit to the needs of corporations in these areas. Even MBEs complain. One MBE reported that when her procurement officer met his total sales-dollar goal for the year, he stopped using minority vendors. Exceeding an annual goal may be seen, unfortunately, as raising expectations for the following year to unrealistic levels.

The least desired criterion for the CPPs was establishing personal relationships. At least two explanations exist. One is the problem of atmosphere noted before, that is, non-minority purchasing personnel are uncomfortable around minorities. A second plausible explanation is that purchasing professional standards require a somewhat dispassionate, arms-length relationship between the parties. However, if the second explanation is to be accepted, this arms-length relationship must be desirable in non-minority relationships, thereby eliminating the possibility that an "old-boy" network exists. Since the "old-boy" network *does* exist, the first explanation may be more plausible.

A more in-depth analysis of the criteria for evaluation was conducted to check for the effects of race and education. This analysis is presented in Table F6 and summarized as follows: Table F6 indicates that race significantly affects the variables of total sales dollars; number of MBEs in the program; helping and developing MBEs; creative uses of MBEs; and increasing buyers' portfolios. In these areas, non-whites supported the evaluation criteria more than whites did, regardless of what group they were in. There were no significant effects for level of education.

Differences due to group (MBE, SBE, and CPP), race, and education are summarized as follows: Differences between the groups were found on almost all the variables, indicating sharp contrasts between the transaction costs facing the three groups. MBEs report higher transaction costs, more willingness to engage in activities to improve MBE purchasing programs, and a more multi-dimensional approach to the evaluation of these programs. Additionally, the respondent's race strongly affected many impediments and activities. Lastly, there were no differences related to the educational level of the respondents.

ANALYSIS OF VARIANCE BY INDUSTRY

The next section explores differences in impediments, activities, and criteria for evaluation based on industry. Eight different two-digit Standard Industrial Classification (SIC) codes were represented in the sample of CPPs. The eight are:

(1) Food and kindred products
(2) Chemicals and allied products
(3) Petroleum products
(4) Stone, clay, glass, and concrete products
(5) Electronics equipment
(6) Transportation equipment
(7) Communications
(8) General merchandise stores

An analysis was conducted to determine if any differences in CPP responses could be attributed to differences in the industry that the CPP worked in. Three separate analyses were conducted, one for the impediments, one for the activities, and one for the criteria for evaluation. The complete analysis of variance tables are presented in Appendix F as Tables F7-F9, and a summary of these results follows.

Table F7 presents the results of an analysis of variance for the impediment variables by industry group. The table shows small but significant differences among industries for the following variables: small numbers, business uncertainty, impacted information, and value similarity. Of these four, only business uncertainty and value similarity show statistical differences between pairs of industries. There is a difference between industry 3 (petroleum prod-

ucts) and industry 7 (communications) on business uncertainty ($p<.05$). The petroleum industry respondents reported higher levels of business uncertainty about the MBEs they did business with than did the communications respondents. The other major statistical difference was that the industry 1 (food products) sample reported higher value similarity than the industry 7 (communications) sample.

Table F8 in Appendix F shows a similar analysis for the activity variables. The only significant overall industry differences for the activity variables are found in monitoring of corporations and searching for MBEs. Differences on the desirability of monitoring CPPs more closely are found between industry 2 (chemicals and allied products) and industries 5, 6, and 7 (electronics equipment, transportation equipment, and communications) ($p<.05$). In each case, personnel in the chemical industry were less likely to see the additional benefits of internal monitoring activities than were personnel in electronics, transportation, and communications industries, respectively. Only one pair of industry differences is significant for the variables concerning searching for MBEs. Again, the personnel in chemicals were less likely than personnel in the electronics industry to see activities in this area as beneficial ($p<.05$).

Table F9 in Appendix F reports the analysis of the criteria for evaluating MBE purchasing programs by industry. Only two of seven main effects are significant across industries: the use of the federal quota system, and establishing personal relationships. Of these, only the federal quota criterion has significant differences between industry groups. Specifically, industry 6 (transportation equipment) favors the use of federal quotas more than does industry 3 (petroleum products) or industry 7 (communications).

In summary, only small differences between industries exist. Overall, these appear to be idiosyncratic and limited to specific pairs of industries. Generally, these eight industries face similar problems, recommend similar activities, and recommend similar methods for evaluating their programs. To the extent that there is dissension about MBE purchasing programs, it exists between the MBE community and the corporate community, not between specific industries.

ANALYSIS OF VARIANCE BY JOB TITLE

Four different job titles within the CPP sample were examined: buyer, manager, corporate staff, and corporate executive. The following analysis identifies differences in the impediments, activities, and criteria for evaluation by job title.

Table F10 in Appendix F reports an analysis of the impediment variables by job title. The only impediment variables that differed by job title are: small numbers, impacted information, and value similarity. The difference between buyers and their managers on the issue of small numbers is significant (p<.05). Managers felt that small numbers of MBEs in desirable areas are more of a problem than their buyers did. However, buyers were affected by the problem of impacted information more than were managers or corporate staff. These results indicate that the problems of MBE purchasing programs are perceived and acted upon differently at different levels of the organization. Additionally, managers reported greater value similarity than did the buyers. This provides evidence that there may be a gap between the managers and the buyers on the importance of business values, which is reflected in how each views the MBE purchasing program.

Table F11 in Appendix F reports the results of the activity variables by job title. Although there is some agreement among job titles concerning the impediments to MBE purchasing programs, there is great disagreement concerning which activities should be included in an MBE program. This is hardly surprising since the costs of implementing these activities fall differently on the representatives of each job title. These, too, are transaction costs. The table shows that there are significant differences on all the activity variables except the provision of financial assistance, which CPPs do not support. (See Appendix E.)

Differences between pairs of job titles (p<.05) exist for: monitoring of corporations and searching for MBEs (managers support more than buyers); searching for CPPs (managers and corporate staff support more than buyers); and managerial assistance (everyone supports more than buyers). For the other activities, buyers are generally the least supportive group. It seems that buyers feel they will be responsible for performing these activities, an extra administrative burden to their already complex jobs. This administrative burden, like the impediments, is a transaction cost. Increments to already high transaction-cost contracting, like MBE purchasing programs, are not supported by those expected to bear the cost. The added cost is why trying harder at already available activities is apparently not the answer. Changes in the structure of the programs may be necessary to promote success.

Table F12 in Appendix F presents the results of an analysis of criteria for evaluation by job title. The only differences in recommended criteria for evaluation by job title concern the creative use of MBEs and increasing the buyer's portfolio of MBEs. The only difference in a comparison between any two variables is for increasing the buyer's portfolio, with the managers as more supportive of this criterion than are the buyers (p<.05).

In summary, differences exist according to the job title of the respondent, within the corporate purchasing personnel sample. While these differences are minor for the impediments and the criteria for evaluation, they are major for the activities. Overall, the trend is that buyers are more likely to see problems in implementing MBE programs and are less likely to recommend activities to overcome these problems. The reasons for this appear to be the already heavy burden of transaction costs on the buyer, and the reluctance to increase this burden with additional activities.

FUTURE RECOMMENDATIONS AND RESEARCH DIRECTIONS •

RECOMMENDATIONS FOR ACTION

This study suggests several new directions for MBE purchasing programs. The first recommendation is to work harder at implementing the programs that already exist. This means addressing the impediments directly and focusing on those activities that *reduce transaction costs* between MBEs and CPPs: reducing complexity; increasing the pool of qualified MBEs; improving the atmosphere for negotiations; encouraging trust while penalizing opportunistic behavior; minimizing business uncertainty; and keeping information lines open in both directions. Many firms already do these things through various mechanisms, but a better job still needs to be done. Designing incentives for purchasing personnel as well as for MBEs is recommended as a means to this end.

A second recommendation is to employ mechanisms to *shift transaction costs* away from the decision makers, namely, the purchasing personnel and the MBE owners. This has the effect of uncoupling the decision to contract from the high costs of executing and monitoring the contract. Since monitoring and execution costs inhibit contracting, this uncoupling should result in more contracting. Administrative units or personnel are needed to absorb these shifted costs. This absorption could take the form of staff specialists outside purchasing, specialists within purchasing but not responsible for contract negotiating, or units outside the firm altogether, such as minority purchasing councils. Effective minority purchasing councils are capable of absorbing these transaction costs (covering the expense with dues and membership fees) and facilitating agreements. They can also provide economies of scale (size) and scope (range of activities) that a single purchasing organization could not achieve.

These two recommendations, to reduce transaction costs and to shift transaction costs, may serve to reduce transaction costs, but that does not mean necessarily that total program costs will be reduced. What the two recommendations suggest is that these program costs be shifted away from the MBEs and CPPs so that better decisions can be made.

A third recommendation addresses the criteria for evaluation results. It is recommended that corporations adopt multiple criteria for evaluating their MBE programs and the performance of their purchasing personnel. Quantitative goals like total sales dollars and the federal quota are useful, but limited. Indeed, sometimes these can be used against promoting minority business because a filled quota is no longer a motivator, and an unattainable dollar figure (in the absence of sanctions) makes people cynical. Qualitative goals and criteria with flexibility that allow many different modes of success are recommended to augment current methods.

The final recommendation is to experiment with some innovative programs suggested by the results of this study. These innovations fall under the heading of "internalization." They require the mixing of corporate and MBE resources, assets, money, and people in a manner that is better than arms-length contracting. Internalization is a way to bring the MBE and corporation together either physically or contractually for a self-defined limited time so that, once the firms are separated and once again legally distinct, *the transaction costs will be permanently reduced.*

A few examples may illustrate this recommendation. An MBE incubator facility would reduce the business- and production-uncertainty transaction costs by providing resources and securing monitoring capability. An incubator facility is an overhead sharing device that allows a number of small businesses to share space costs, administrative overhead, and specialist employees. With corporate financial assistance and monitoring, an incubator would enable CPPs to directly observe the progress of the MBEs and enable the MBEs immediate access to corporate personnel and information. The MBEs would no longer be outsiders who had to overcome all the barriers of selling to a large corporation.

A more revolutionary suggestion is to develop a "repurchasing agreement" for the minority-owned business. This would entail having the corporation literally buy the MBE for a limited time, with contractual responsibilities for the repurchasing of the MBE firm by the minority owner. During the time of corporate ownership, the minority owner would be a salaried employee of the corporation in a vendor/consulting role. While the MBE is owned by the corporation it is no longer an outsider but an insider. During this time many of the transaction-cost barriers could be overcome. At a prearranged time for a prearranged price, the MBE would repurchase the business. All the internal efficiencies that were developed could be exploited to lower the transaction costs of doing business.

A final example of internalization is a program analogous to affirmative-action recruiting of college students. In this case, however, minority students would be recruited for special training with the goal of eventually pursuing an entrepreneurial opportunity. During the minority person's training, he/she would be exposed to the corporation's operations that were best suited to MBE procurement. Then, when the trainee leaves the corporation, that individual is well-qualified to act as a supplier to his/her prior employer. While it is recognized that this program is relatively expensive, it serves the purpose of lowering the transaction costs of later procurement.

FUTURE RESEARCH

One area for future research is an investigation similar to the one described in this study but with a better control group. A national sample, better matched to MBEs, would definitively answer the questions concerning the effect of size versus race. The results here suggest that on some issues race is the most important variable, and on others it is the size of the small business.

A second concern still to be investigated is that of women-owned businesses. Again, a transaction-cost framework could be employed and the differences based on women's ownership explored.

A final area for future research is in the area of MBE performance. This study did not employ a dependent performance variable and attempt to predict which MBEs would be most successful because of their corporate relationships. However, this is clearly important to the design of MBE programs. MBE programs that facilitate transactions but do so at the expense of the MBEs do not achieve the overriding goal of MBE economic development.

APPENDIX A: THE APPLICATION OF TRANSACTION COST ECONOMICS TO THE PROBLEMS OF MINORITY BUSINESS PURCHASING •

STUDY FRAMEWORK: IMPEDIMENTS AS TRANSACTION COSTS

The transaction-cost framework was developed and elaborated by Williamson (1975, 1981) based upon earlier work by Coase (1937), Simon (1957), March and Simon (1958), and Thompson (1967), among others. It focuses on the "transaction" as the basic unit of economic activity. A transaction can be defined as the transfer of goods and services between technologically separate units (Williamson, 1981; Walker and Weber, 1984) and "transaction costs" can be defined as the costs associated with exchange that vary independent of the prices of the goods and services sold (Robins, 1987). Examples of the applications of transaction cost economics include: problems of vertical integration (Anderson, 1982), make-or-buy decisions (Walker and Weber, 1984), internal labor markets (Williamson, 1975), property rights and organizational culture (Jones, 1983).

Transaction cost economics (TCE) views markets and firms as alternatives for completing transactions. If transaction costs are too high, deals are too expensive to make, and markets become inefficient and fail. If this should occur, the rationality of efficiency dictates that the transaction then should take place within the firm. This explanation of the substitution of hierarchy (intrafirm transfers) for markets is seen as the major contribution of the TCE approach and has helped to integrate the fields of microeconomics and organizational theory (Ouchi, 1977; Williamson, 1981).

The TCE theory of market failure notes that the costs of contracting across a market vary by three factors: the human decision makers, the properties of the markets (environmental factors), and the internal structures of the firms. Under certain conditions, combinations of the human and environmental elements lead to market failure or the realization that the use of the market for transactions is irrationally inefficient. When market failure occurs, the pressure of rationality causes the firm to retreat from the market and transact the exchange internally through the use of hierarchy.

The human factors that lead to market failure are the conditions of bounded rationality and opportunism. Bounded rationality refers to the limits people experience in formulating and solving complex problems and in processing information. People intend to behave rationally but are limited. Complexity overcomes their rationality and they simply do the best they can. Opportunism is behavior that is self-interested with guile. People who make self-disbelieved statements, false and empty promises, are behaving opportunistically.

The environmental factors are the presence of small numbers of firms and performance (or volume) uncertainty. Williamson (1981) described how the pairing of uncertainty with bounded rationality and of small numbers with opportunism lead to inefficient contracting and high transaction costs, thereby making contracting impossible. Walker and Weber (1984) argued that the mere presence of a condition was sufficient for market failure and that the "pairings" of Williamson were not required.

The context and experience of MBE purchasing programs reflect the presence of all four factors mentioned above: bounded rationality, opportunism, small numbers, and performance uncertainty. Although the literature on MBE purchasing is limited, a few scholars and practitioners have discussed these problems. Bounded rationality is a problem for both the MBE vendor and the corporate purchasing agent. Of course, the purchasing function is complex even without MBE purchasing goals (Leenders, Fearon, and England, 1985). However, more complexity is injected into the purchasing function when purchasing personnel have the additional burden of meeting MBE purchasing goals for salary review and of finding qualified vendors through intermediary organizations like the National Minority Supplier Development Council (Dowst, 1981). Practitioners have noted that standard operating procedures for procurement require adjustment to deal with the MBE problem. The provision of technical and managerial assistance is recommended (Simpson, 1982) but is often beyond the control of the buyer. Affirmative procurement, taking positive, creative steps beyond the ordinary (Williams, 1988), is suggested but clearly places additional demands on buyer rationality.

Two additional factors are hypothesized by Williamson (1975) as affecting transaction costs. These are "information impactedness" and "atmosphere." Information impactedness is a derivative condition that arises mainly from uncertainty and opportunism but is related to bounded rationality as well. It emerges as a factor when parties to a transaction have information that each other needs, but they do not share it. Both sides to the MBE purchasing equation have this problem. Corporations have large purchasing needs spread throughout many divisions and geographic areas. Buyers have both specific and general responsibilities for procurement. Often, in soliciting bid quotes, time is of the essence. The distribution of this information to a small population of firms in mostly fragmented industries is a costly exercise. Similarly, the MBE has limited resources to advertise products and performance, search for opportunities, submit quotes and bids, and negotiate contracts. For both sides, getting the word out is a costly and time-consuming process.

Atmosphere refers to the attitude that people have about doing business with each other. Although this attitude, in an economic sense, should be separate from the transaction, attitude inseparability is a fact of life. To the extent that doing business with someone is unpleasant, a cost is incurred by the parties. The inclusion of the atmosphere dimension enables this study to account for the "social embeddedness" of these transactions and the possibilities of racial and cultural bias.

To summarize the transaction-costs framework for this study, six general dimensions or variables can impede the success of MBE purchasing programs: *relatively small numbers of MBEs; bounded rationality of decision-makers; performance uncertainty; opportunism; information impactedness;* and *atmosphere*. In addition, a set of variables that is not in the transaction-costs framework but is related to it, *resource dependence, value importance,* and *value similarity*, was included in the study. Resource dependence refers to the extent to which the firm relies on other firms for its survival. Value importance is a variable that taps the salience of "values," and value similarity is the extent to which individuals agree on values.

STUDY FRAMEWORK: ACTIVITIES DESIGNED TO OVERCOME IMPEDIMENTS

MBEs have much to gain by lowering the transaction costs that inhibit the success of MBE purchasing programs. MBEs tend to look more favorably than do corporate purchasing personnel on the policies, procedures, and activities that remove, shift, delay, or mitigate the incurring of transaction costs by MBEs. Typically, these policies and activities have the effect of incurring costs for the corporation. Corporate buyers and purchasing personnel will also favor these policies and activities but only to the extent that they shift costs away from the individual buyer and onto another administrative unit. That unit may be somewhere else in the organization, or outside the organization, such as a governmental agency that certifies minority status. These activities fall into five general categories: (1) *monitoring activities;* (2) *searching activities;* (3) *activities designed to improve performance quality;* (4) *activities designed to mitigate the atmosphere problem by providing cultural interaction;* and (5) *the activities that internalize to some degree the MBE/corporate relationship.*

THE RELATIONSHIP BETWEEN IMPEDIMENTS AND ACTIVITIES

The problems of bounded rationality and complexity are reduced by the quasi-internalization of the MBE/corporate relationship. This means that the corporation and the MBEs should work closer together, closer than the usual arms-length contracting relationship. Complete internalization is not feasible because of the rules of the federal orders. The corporation cannot, therefore, permanently and irrevocably take the minority firm over. Of course, complexity is not actually reduced by internalization but shifted away from the market, where it is more difficult to manage. Examples of quasi-internalization include: providing MBEs access to internal training, participation in MBE venture capital pools, and joint ventures.

Performance uncertainty is directly addressed by activities designed to assure quality. These activities may include pre-bid certifications, post-award quality-assurance training, or ongoing technical assistance. In addition, monitoring activities will also help reduce performance uncertainty and enable the parties to make corrections over the life of the contract.

The problems of small-numbers contracting and impacted information are both decreased by activities designed to bring the corporations and MBEs together and disseminate information. By increasing the pool of MBEs with which to do business, the buyer improves the probability of having a price-competitive vendor but also improves the recontracting or renegotiation situation. The buyer with a larger pool of MBEs will be less likely to incur switching costs after the first contract is executed, if the MBE incumbent raises prices or lowers quality. Generally, the larger the pool, the more competitive the market.

Similarly, small numbers and impacted information are reduced by activities that partly internalize the transaction costs. The use of some form of partial internal governance reduces the barriers around communicating contract information and performance data. The problems of both small numbers and recontracting are mitigated by longer-term contracts, shared resources and technical assistance, and provision of financial aid.

The possibility of opportunism increases transaction costs by requiring additional monitoring and search activities to maintain discipline and to replace opportunistic individuals. In addition, the presence of opportunism will suggest internalization as a solution. Internal governance can prevent opportunism by changing the incentives and can enforce discipline through the use of the personnel function, as opposed to the courts.

Lastly, the transaction costs of atmosphere reduce efficiency by allowing bias in the personal relationships between the parties to influence economic decisions. Search activities help to reduce this racial and cultural bias by increasing the interactions between CPPs and MBEs. Activities designed to directly reduce bias, such as the use of minority purchasing agents, can also overcome the atmosphere problem. Internalization can be a positive activity, too. By internalizing the MBE firm to some extent, shared values can develop, and increased contact and interaction are likely to occur.

REFERENCES

Anderson, E. 1982. "The salesperson as outside agent or employee: A transaction cost analysis." Working paper No. 82-027, Wharton School, University of Pennsylvania.

Bates, T. 1985. "Impact of preferential procurement policies on minority-owned businesses." *The Review of Black Political Economy*, 14, 51-65.

Bates, T. and Furino, A. 1985. "A new nationwide data base for minority business." *Journal of Small Business Management*, 23, 41-52.

Coase, R. 1937. "The nature of the firm." 386-405 in *Readings in Price Theory*, (1952) Stigler and Boulding (eds.). Homewood, Illinois: Irwin.

Dowst, S. 1981. "Sure route to better minority sourcing." *Purchasing*, October 8, 77-81.

Giunipero, L. 1980. "Differences between minority and non-minority suppliers." *Journal of Purchasing and Materials Management*, 16, 2-8.

Jones, G. 1983. "Transaction costs, property rights and organizational culture: An exchange perspective." *Administrative Science Quarterly*, 28, 454-467.

____. 1987. "Organization-client transactions and organizational governance structures." *Academy of Management Journal*, 30, 197-218.

Leenders, M., Fearon, H. and England, W. 1985. *Purchasing and Materials Management*. Homewood, Illinois: Irwin.

March, J. and Simon, H. 1958. *Organizations*. New York: Wiley.

Ouchi, W. 1977. "Review of *Markets and Hierarchies*." *Administrative Science Quarterly*, 22, 541-544.

Robins, J. 1987. "Organizational economics: Notes on the use of transaction cost theory in the study of organizations." *Administrative Science Quarterly*, 32, 68-86.

Simon, H. 1957. *Models of Man*. New York: Wiley.

Spratlen, T. 1978. "The impact of affirmative action purchasing." *Journal of Purchasing and Materials Management*, 14, 8-11.

Simpson, R. 1982. "Disadvantaged business purchasing programs." Unpublished master's thesis, University of Colorado, Denver.

Thompson, J. 1967. *Organizations in Action*. New York: McGraw-Hill.

Walker, G. and Weber, D. 1984. "Transaction cost approach to make or buy decisions." *Administrative Science Quarterly*, 29, 373-391.

Williams, R. 1988. "A buyer's guide to doing business with minority vendors." *Proceedings of the National Association of Purchasing Management*, Nashville, Tenn., 228-240.

Williamson, O. 1975. *Markets and Hierarchies.* New York: Free Press.

___. 1981. "The economics of organization: The transaction cost approach." *American Journal of Sociology,* 87, 548-577.

APPENDIX B: RESULTS OF THE FIELD INTERVIEWS   •

GROUNDING THE THEORY: DATA FROM THE FIELD INTERVIEWS

The problems of complexity and bounded rationality emerged from our interviews with vendors from minority businesses. Interviewees repeatedly referred to the complexity of dealing with corporate bureaucracy and details of the bidding process. MBEs cited the additional business complexity caused by slow-paying corporate accounts and the technical complexity of meeting quality specifications.

Both corporate buyers and MBEs were able to provide examples of opportunism in MBE purchasing programs. MBEs were sensitive to false promises made by buyers for contracts, loans, and technical assistance. Buyers, on their part, often mentioned MBE attempts to obtain contracts solely because of their minority status. There was also a sensitivity to the MBE as a front for a non-minority firm. Direct examples of overcharging, theft, and falsified invoices were given.

The two environmental factors that raise transaction costs are the small number of MBE firms in the marketplace and the variability and uncertainty of performance. Again, both these conditions were frequent themes of the interviewees' descriptions of their experiences in MBE purchasing programs. Corporate buyers described serious problems of finding enough MBEs to meet their goals. A particular problem was the small number of high-tech firms. Also noted was the concentration of MBE firms in certain geographic areas and the difficulty of locating MBEs outside areas with large minority populations.

MBEs also saw small numbers as a problem. They agreed that there were too few MBE firms in technical areas and too many in service areas. However, the MBEs placed some of the responsibility on the corporations. MBEs talked about the lack of development assistance from corporations, the lack of financing for larger-scale MBE firms, and the uncertainty of large-volume orders that could insure MBE survival and growth. Additionally, MBEs voiced concern that when buyers had met their goals or quotas for the period, they stopped purchasing from MBEs and returned to their "old-boy-network" suppliers.

The second environmental dimension was performance uncertainty. Both MBEs and corporate buyers raised concerns about the reliability of each other's performance. A theme of the corporate interviews was the uncertain quality of MBE work, primarily in manufacturing areas. Slipped delivery timetables, poor quality assemblies, and high rework rates were often mentioned. The best MBE relationships that corporate buyers could recall were ones where quality was never an issue. A repeated observation was that high-quality MBE performance was often delivered by a former minority employee who was now self-employed. This finding is consistent with TCE theory in that transactions with former employees may closely resemble prior hierarchical transactions. Contracting with former employees lowers transaction costs to the extent that standards and operating procedures are internalized by the former employee.

Similarly, MBEs noted performance and volume uncertainty in their dealings with corporate MBE programs. MBE interviewees reported irregular orders and bidding specifications, slow payment, and changes in specifications and volume *after* bids had been accepted. A number of MBEs noticed that turnover in the purchasing function was high, and this made it difficult to predict if the personal relationships established with one purchasing agent would carry over to the new buyer.

Two additional factors are hypothesized by Williamson (1975) as affecting transaction costs. These are "information impactedness" and "atmosphere." Information impactedness is a derivative condition that arises mainly from uncertainty and opportunism but is related to bounded rationality as well. It emerges as a factor when one party to a transaction has information that is material to the other party, but which it cannot impart without cost. Both sides to the MBE purchasing equation have this problem. Corporations have large purchasing needs spread throughout many divisions and geographic areas. Buyers have both specific and general responsibilities for procurement. Often in soliciting bid quotes, time is of the essence. The distribution of this information to a small number of firms in mostly fragmented industries is a costly exercise. Similarly, the MBE has limited resources to advertise products and performance, search for opportunities, submit quotes and bids, and negotiate contracts. For both sides, getting the word out is a costly and time-consuming process.

Atmosphere refers to the attitude people have about doing business with each other. Although this attitude, in an economic sense, should be separate from the transaction, attitude inseparability is a fact of life. To the extent that doing business with someone is unpleasant, a cost is incurred by the parties. Although only one corporate interviewee would admit to the probability of racial and cultural bias at his firm, buyers would frequently refer to an occasional "give-me" attitude by an MBE salesperson making a "hard-sell" pitch about filling federal quotas. MBEs were more sensitive to the atmosphere issue and almost unanimously reported that they sensed an undercurrent of bias. They felt that the purchasing agent's reluctance to help their firms was the result of prejudice.

CORPORATE INTERVIEWS: SUMMARY

Level of Interview

Level of Interview (C) (D) (L)
C=corporate HQ, D=divisional location, L=line person (buyer)

Food products: Corp. VP, Minority Purchasing (C)
Pharmaceuticals: Staff Purchasing (L)
Chemicals: Purchasing Manager, Research Div. (D)
Telecommunications: Corp. Minority/SB Program Adm. (C)
Automotive: Plant Purchasing Mgr. & Buyer (L)
Cable TV system operator: Corp. EEOC/MBE Coordinator (C)
Petroleum products: Buyer/Research Div. (L)
Defense contractor: Chief of Business Utilization, Astronautics (D)
Computer manufacturer: Coordinator, MBE programs (D)
Computer manufacturer: Buyer and SB coordinator (L)
Electronics manufacturer: SB/Disadvantaged Mgr. (D)
Computer manufacturer: Minority Vendor Representative (D)
Pharmaceuticals: SB/MBE Administrator (C)

Totals   (C) = 4   (D) = 5   (L) = 4

Program Initiation

In response to federal requirements: Defense Department, Federal Communications Commission, Interior Department, Food and Drug Administration, Agriculture Department . . . others.

As a result of a merger with a firm that has a developed program of commitment.

Initiated by a buyer in the field with a personal interest.

Pre-federal voluntary from corporate headquarters: small business commitment, economic development, social concern, public awareness.

Program Implementation

Top-management support mostly. Takes many forms.

Formal policies mostly. Not updated regularly.

Centralized reporting and monitoring:
    Often a corporate officer/staff coordinator;
    Not all departments use central purchasing function;
    Can be structured as profit center with strong leadership.

Division level goals—sometimes met by single vendor.

Individual goals: MBO (dollars, numbers, and percentages):
    Lots of buyer discretion still possible;
    Some have no goals;
    Some local emphasis.

Communications: memos, vendor lists, reports, brochures:
    Some attempt at more public visibility.

Incentives rarely used, sanctions rarely enforced, audits seldom done:
    Commendations, raises possible.

Selection process—most require certification:
    Price, quality, service, delivery primary;
    Sources of contacts—directories, local MBE purchasing councils, fairs and shows;
    Qualified and qualifiable;
    Try to flag and monitor early.

Areas of usage:
    Services: cleaning, metal fabrication, woodwork, common carriers;
    Office supply and equipment;
    Printing/consulting;
    Few commodity-type products: bags, chocolate, circuit boards;
    (Need in high-tech areas).

Economic development:
    Local MBE purchasing councils/TRIAD;
    Tuck School scholarships.

Measuring effectiveness:
    Goal attainment (total dollars, numbers in program);
    Developmental goals;
    Problem resolutions;
    Training MBEs.

Positive Experiences

Professional performance, soft-sell, good personal relationships.
Developed and aided after a fire, great supplier, president's commitment.
MBE showed patience, received development help, showed firm how to work with it.
Provided MBE with complete business services, put MBE in business, continues to be only customer. Total development effort.
Professional with high degree of technical know-how. Easy to do business with.
Good personal relationships, worked through local MBE council. High-quality work.
Ex-employee started business, knew firm and expectations.
R & D grant aided firm development, high quality follows. Gets on team early.
Vendor quality improved through firm engineering, willingness to listen.
Engineering development, team effort, great service and support.
Chemical distributor—soft-sell, professional, electronic order transmission.

Negative Experiences

Hostile attitude, poor performance.
SBA referral, buyer resistance, complaints w/o resolution. MBE hard-sell.
Poor performance, couldn't deliver . . . just like any bad vendor.
Poor bidding record. Complaint by minority about MBE status. Caused huge paper trail.

Quotas too high to reach in municipalities; fronts and middlemen exploit, bureaucrats operate businesses.
Prices too low, poor workmanship and delivery.
Overcharging and opportunism.
Failure to meet specs, poor quality.
Hard-sell MBEs, refuse to correct specs, poor quality.
Theft from housekeeping service, bad attitudes concerning entitlement.
Management incompetence after development efforts.

Impediments to Success

MBE Problems:
> The give-me attitude by MBEs.
> Hiding management and financial disabilities by MBEs.
> Politicizing the program by MBEs.
> MBEs clustered in a few industries; lack of high-tech.
> Uncertain performance.
> Poor bidding practices—too low.
> Undercapitalized.
> Some firms exploit minority status.

Corporate Problems:
> Stress and conflict in buyers.
> Vendors disillusioned by corporate bureaucracy.
> Negativism by buyers towards minorities.
> Subcontractors impossible to monitor.
> No incentives for buyers.
> Distributors and wholesalers blocked by national agreements.
> Union prevents subcontracting at times.
> Corporations sometimes very slow to pay.
> Developmental efforts (resources) not available.
> No imagination.
> High costs of identifying and qualifying firms.
> Corporate buyers need to integrate through team approach.
> Association with an MBE program is a stigma.
> Buyer turnover too fast for relationships to develop.
> Rationalization of purchasing preempts efforts.

Rule Changes Needed

Percentage goals too high and unrealistic.
Too much paperwork.
No monitoring/auditing leads to abuses.
Quotas can lead to inequities, steering.
Standardize certification process and monitor to prevent cheating.
Mandatory programs lead to hard-sell tactics.
Monitoring of subcontracts (required) too costly, not done.
Set-asides not professional purchasing practice.

Tools that Work

Local minority business councils.
Management assistance.
Strong leadership from designated MBE/SB coordinator.

In-person contact and relationships.
Internal communication capability.
Engineering assistance.
Materials management and purchasing assistance.
Prepayment agreements.
Fairs and trade shows.
Directories.
Team approach to vendor relations.
Computer monitoring.
Nonbusiness get-togethers to develop relationships.

Types of Minority Businesses Interviewed

Battery supplier (auto and medical).
Medical emergency repair.
Small computers and supplies.
Filter sales and service (heating, ventilation, and air conditioning).
Personal computers/consulting.
Advertising specialties.
Electronics assembly.
Economic development/manpower consultant.
Engineering and testing services.
Electronics supply house.

Measures of MBE Program Effectiveness

Personal contact and feedback.
Dollars spent as a percentage of total procurement.
Number of black buyers.
Develop relationships; get feedback.
Number of start-ups and successes.
Size of MBE vendor base.
Ability to meet quotas.
Consistency of policy.

Positive Experiences

Long-term relationship develops into big contract.
Positive personal contact leads to high-margin, prompt-payment deal.
Long-term relationship progresses along with professional conduct.
Postal service director fronts seed money/development costs to finish project.
Growing relationship . . . larger contracts over time.
No positive experiences (economic development/manpower consultant).
Regional MDSC has really opened doors.
Large company adopts MBE and helps it develop.
Mayor intervenes on government contract to expedite payment.

Negative Experiences

Government officials bureaucratize a system that worked well.
Asian reports blacks discriminated against him because he had no black employees.
Reneged on promise of loan, caused severe financial pressure.

DOD reneged on promises of funding, almost caused bankruptcy.
Large company with high community visibility, but does nothing.
Sent computer lists of commodities without explanations.
Believes company stopped doing business when they found out he was black.
Believes lower-level buyers resist mandates from above.
Believes majority companies very complacent about goals and MBEs.
Believes a buyer tried to embarrass him with too large a contract.
Shipments rejected without explanation.
Heard stories of hidden biases and racism.

Impediments

Financing, financing, financing.
Lack of commitment from corporations.
MBEs too impotent to reverse trend or negotiate.
Too hard to get doors opened.
No support structure for MBEs, must meet standard rules.
Cultural and racial misunderstandings.
"Old-boy" networks exclude minorities.
Late payments.
Small volumes.
— Accepts unreasonably low bids.

Government Rules

Bonding on construction contracts restrictive.
Government is slow to pay.
— MBEs try to be things they are not . . . do too many things. Laws push too fast, more development needed.
Quotas are often used as maximums, not minimums.
Paperwork and regulations add to costs.
"Set asides" are dirty words . . . MBEs face stigma of special treatment.
— Can't legislate fairness, understanding.
Better enforcement.
Government bureaucracy is hopeless.

Suggested Solutions: What Works

CEO involvement and monitoring.
Individual incentives for buyers. But don't cause resentment.
— Personal contact. Tour facilities. Both ways.
— Get MBEs additional training.
Make MBEs part of the procurement team. Early involvement.
MBEs must learn to sell themselves. Become visible and professional.
— Develop MBEs slowly. Adopt MBEs.
— Must be willing to reach out to MBEs.
Communicate accurate information to MBEs. Avoid platitudes.
Corporations should recognize that discrimination exists, be sensitive and aware.
Assess and monitor compliance.
— Hire black buyers.
Identify opportunities for social interaction.
Help with financing (debt and equity), early payments.
MBEs need longer lead times, sometimes.

MINORITY BUSINESSES INTERVIEW GUIDE (sample)

Interview Introduction

The purpose of this interview, as I indicated over the phone, is to assist the Center for Advanced Purchasing Studies (CAPS) to find ways to improve the working relationships between MBEs and corporate purchasing departments so that there will be greater involvement of MBEs in large corporate programs.

A necessary first step in this process is to try to determine the problems that firms are having and identify some of the solutions they have tried. While various individuals have indicated that working relationships should be improved, a systematic assessment of what should be done has not been conducted.

Therefore, for this project, we have reviewed other studies and examined information on this topic and are conducting interviews with MBEs and corporate purchasing agents and buyers.

Your firm is one of about twenty we randomly selected from the *Try Us '88* directory throughout the country. Since it is impractical to interview everyone, we are relying on a sample of interviews with representative firms. As such, we are most interested in your experiences and suggestions. If you have reliable information based on other minority business firms' experience, I will be glad to hear about them, too.

None of your comments today will be reported to anyone using either your name or your firm's name, nor will your comments in any way be identifiable. All our interviews will be disguised and aggregated. Therefore, we assure you that your responses will be held in strictest confidence; we encourage you to be as frank as possible.

Background Information

A. Type of business _____

B. Number of employees _____

C. Sales ($):
    1. 0-200,000   2. 200,001-400,000
    3. 400,001-600,000   4. 600,001-800,000
    5. 800,001-1,000,000 6. 1,000,001-1,200,000
    7. 1,200,001-1,400,000 8. Over 1,400,000

D. Percentage of total sales attributed to MBE status:
    1. 0-25%   2. 26-50%   3. 51-75%   4. 76-100%

E. How long have you been in business? _____

F. Do you now do business with a previous employer? _____

G. Are you certified by some agency? _____ If so, by whom? _____

H. How many direct (prime) contracts did you bid on last year? _____
                                  Subcontracts? _____

I. About what percentage of contracts bid on have been awarded?
   Prime? _____   Subcontracts? _____

J. How would you characterize your firm's relationships with large corporate purchasing departments and MBE programs?

1	2	3	4	5
unsatisfactory	somewhat unsatisfactory	satisfactory	somewhat successful	successful

K. What are the best ways to measure the effectiveness of corporate MBE programs?

L. What are the best ways to measure the MBE's effectiveness?

General Questions

A. Based on your experience (or information from a reliable source), describe examples of any positive working relations you have had with corporate purchasing departments, purchasing agents, or MBE purchasing programs.

Describe specifically why it was a positive working relationship. For example, describe the circumstances and what exactly happened that was positive.

B. Based on your experience (or information from a reliable source), describe examples of any negative working relations you have had with corporate purchasing departments, purchasing agents, or MBE purchasing programs.

Describe specifically why it was a negative working relationship. For example, describe the circumstances and what exactly happened that was negative.

C. Based upon your experiences, what are the most important reasons why corporate purchasing/MBE working relationships are not always successful? Also describe why subcontractor relations are not always successful.

D. Should the federal, state, and local rules (programs and laws) for dealing with MBEs be changed? If yes, how?

E. What are the most significant impediments (hurdles) in your view to successfully doing business with larger corporate purchasing departments, purchasing agents, or MBE programs? What could be done to minimize or overcome these impediments?

F. What is the most helpful tool/aspect of an MBE program you have experienced in doing business with purchasing departments, purchasing agents, or MBE purchasing programs?

APPENDIX C: COVER LETTERS AND SURVEY •

Dear *Try Us '88* Supplier:

A major study has been undertaken aimed at identifying the impediments to Minority Business Enterprise Purchasing programs and uncovering possible solutions to these problems. You have been selected from the *Try Us '88* directory as a representative minority-owned firm in your industry. I am writing to urge you to participate in the study by completing the enclosed questionnaire. It will only take a few minutes to complete.

The study is being conducted by Indiana University under the auspices of the Center for Advanced Purchasing Studies and the National Association of Purchasing Management. The study is sponsored by a number of large corporations who wish to assess and improve their efforts in the minority purchasing area. We have developed a questionnaire that asks your personal opinion about minority purchasing programs and company-related matters. There are no right or wrong answers, and this is not a test. The information you provide will be seen only by the researchers, and the results will be presented in summary form.

Enclosed is a survey and a self-addressed, postage-paid envelope. I urge you to take a few minutes and complete the survey. Be completely honest and candid, and answer the questions to the best of your ability. Your responses are completely confidential.

Once you have completed the survey, please put it in the enclosed self-addressed, postage-paid envelope, seal it, and mail it by **September 1**. If you have any questions about the survey, you may contact me (call collect) at 812-335-8529 at Indiana University.

I urge you to participate. The results of the study should make MBE purchasing programs more effective and aid the corporate community in becoming more sensitive to the MBE community.

Thank you for your effort.

Sincerely,

Marc J. Dollinger, Ph.D.
Research Director

SAMPLE COVER LETTER FOR MBE PURCHASING STUDY

Dear Employees:

We at [company name] have agreed to participate in a major study aimed at identifying the impediments to Minority Business Enterprise Purchasing programs and uncovering possible solutions to these problems.

The study is being conducted by Dr. Marc J. Dollinger of Indiana University under the auspices of the Center for Advanced Purchasing Studies and the National Association of Purchasing Management. We have invited Dr. Dollinger to help assess and improve our efforts in the minority purchasing area. He has developed a questionnaire that asks your personal opinion about minority purchasing programs and company-related matters. There are no right or wrong answers, and this is not a test. The information you provide will be seen only by the researchers, and the results will be presented in summary form.

Enclosed is a survey and a self-addressed, postage-paid envelope. I urge you to take a few minutes and complete the survey. Be completely honest and candid, and answer the questions to the best of your ability. Your responses are completely confidential.

Once you have completely filled out the survey, please put it in the enclosed self-addressed, stamped envelope, seal it, and mail it by [two weeks from date of distribution]. If you have any questions about the surveys, you may contact [corporate contact person] or Dr. Dollinger, 812-335-8529 at Indiana University.

I urge you to participate. The results of the study should enable us to improve our MBE purchasing programs and aid us in becoming more sensitive to the MBE community. The more surveys returned from [company name], the more reliable the results will be. Our commitment to the minority community and to equal opportunity is strong and unflagging, and we wish to do our part to improve the effort.

Thank you for your effort.

Sincerely,

[High-level executive]

MINORITY BUSINESS ENTERPRISE PURCHASING PROGRAM SURVEY

The purpose of this survey is to investigate some of the issues of Minority Business Enterprise (MBE) purchasing programs and the potential solutions to these problems. Your cooperation is vital. Please answer all of the questions as best you can. Your answers are completely **confidential**; only the researchers at the Center for Advanced Purchasing Studies and Indiana University will see this survey. Thank you for your help.

Instructions: On the following pages are statements used to describe problems of Minority Business Enterprise (MBE) purchasing programs. Read each statement carefully and think about your own company. Then indicate whether you (1) **Strongly Disagree**, (2) **Moderately Disagree**, (3) **Slightly Disagree**, (4) **Neither Agree nor Disagree**, (5) **Slightly Agree**, (6) **Moderately Agree**, or (7) **Strongly Agree** with the statement by circling the appropriate number next to the statement.

1 STRONGLY DISAGREE	2 MODERATELY DISAGREE	3 SLIGHTLY DISAGREE	4 NEITHER AGREE NOR DISAGREE	5 SLIGHTLY AGREE	6 MODERATELY AGREE	7 STRONGLY AGREE

1.	Doing business with large corporations is not very profitable for MBEs.	1 2 3 4 5 6 7
2.	Finding contracts to bid is time-consuming for MBEs.	1 2 3 4 5 6 7
3.	MBEs have difficulty advertising their products/services.	1 2 3 4 5 6 7
4.	Corporations apply their purchasing regulations inconsistently.	1 2 3 4 5 6 7
5.	It is difficult for MBEs to get information from corporations.	1 2 3 4 5 6 7
6.	Corporations don't get the word out about their MBE programs.	1 2 3 4 5 6 7
7.	It is hard to match the MBE firm with the corporation's need.	1 2 3 4 5 6 7
8.	The designation of "minority business" hurts MBEs.	1 2 3 4 5 6 7
9.	Subcontractors don't help MBEs.	1 2 3 4 5 6 7
10.	MBEs can't compete with bigger firms.	1 2 3 4 5 6 7
11.	Buyers don't know much about minority-owned firms.	1 2 3 4 5 6 7
12.	MBEs need technical assistance.	1 2 3 4 5 6 7
13.	Buyers are inconsistent in implementing the MBE program.	1 2 3 4 5 6 7
14.	Buyers use MBEs just to satisfy statistics.	1 2 3 4 5 6 7
15.	Buyers don't work closely with MBEs.	1 2 3 4 5 6 7
16.	Corporations don't give much feedback to MBEs.	1 2 3 4 5 6 7
17.	Corporations take too long to pay.	1 2 3 4 5 6 7
18.	It's hard for MBEs to get their foot in the door.	1 2 3 4 5 6 7
19.	MBEs become disillusioned with corporate bureaucracy.	1 2 3 4 5 6 7
20.	MBEs are often undercapitalized.	1 2 3 4 5 6 7
21.	There is a lack of corporate commitment to MBE purchasing programs.	1 2 3 4 5 6 7
22.	MBEs are powerless to negotiate favorable terms.	1 2 3 4 5 6 7
23.	Cultural misunderstandings hurt MBE purchasing programs.	1 2 3 4 5 6 7
24.	MBEs need long lead times to correct quality problems.	1 2 3 4 5 6 7
25.	Buyers rely on their "old-boy networks" for supplies.	1 2 3 4 5 6 7
26.	Only small-volume orders are placed with MBEs.	1 2 3 4 5 6 7
27.	The government doesn't enforce the regulations on MBE purchasing.	1 2 3 4 5 6 7
28.	Lead times for MBE quotes are too short.	1 2 3 4 5 6 7
29.	Lead times for MBE deliveries are too short.	1 2 3 4 5 6 7
30.	MBEs are not available in specialized areas.	1 2 3 4 5 6 7
31.	Buyers are not aware of available MBEs.	1 2 3 4 5 6 7
32.	MBEs don't expand their businesses to meet corporate needs.	1 2 3 4 5 6 7
33.	MBEs are naive/inexperienced with the corporate world.	1 2 3 4 5 6 7
34.	MBEs are not price-competitive.	1 2 3 4 5 6 7
35.	Buyers lack information on MBE capability.	1 2 3 4 5 6 7
36.	MBEs can't handle the paperwork.	1 2 3 4 5 6 7
37.	MBEs can't meet bid/quote deadlines.	1 2 3 4 5 6 7
38.	MBEs hide problems that they are having.	1 2 3 4 5 6 7
39.	Racial biases hurt MBE purchasing programs.	1 2 3 4 5 6 7

1	2	3	4	5	6	7
STRONGLY DISAGREE	MODERATELY DISAGREE	SLIGHTLY DISAGREE	NEITHER AGREE NOR DISAGREE	SLIGHTLY AGREE	MODERATELY AGREE	STRONGLY AGREE

40. Buyers have no incentive to make MBE purchasing program work. 1 2 3 4 5 6 7
41. MBEs have a "give-me" attitude. 1 2 3 4 5 6 7
42. The MBE purchasing program is all politics. 1 2 3 4 5 6 7
43. MBEs are clustered in a few industry areas. 1 2 3 4 5 6 7
44. MBEs are clustered in a few geographic areas. 1 2 3 4 5 6 7
45. Performance by MBEs is too uncertain. 1 2 3 4 5 6 7
46. MBEs have poor bidding practices. 1 2 3 4 5 6 7
47. Buyers feel stress and conflict reaching MBE purchasing goals. 1 2 3 4 5 6 7
48. MBEs have inefficient production capacities. 1 2 3 4 5 6 7
49. Subcontractors are impossible to monitor. 1 2 3 4 5 6 7
50. MBE distributor and wholesale business blocked by national agreements. 1 2 3 4 5 6 7
51. Unions prevent subcontracting to MBEs. 1 2 3 4 5 6 7
52. Corporate resources to develop MBEs are not available. 1 2 3 4 5 6 7
53. Corporations don't have the imagination to make MBE programs work. 1 2 3 4 5 6 7
54. Identifying and qualifying MBEs is a costly process. 1 2 3 4 5 6 7
55. Individual buyers are out on their own when it comes to MBE programs. 1 2 3 4 5 6 7
56. High buyer turnover hurts long-term relationships with MBEs. 1 2 3 4 5 6 7
57. MBE purchasing programs are at odds with efficient purchasing practice. 1 2 3 4 5 6 7
58. MBE programs lead buyers to compromise their professional standards. 1 2 3 4 5 6 7
59. MBEs have high failure rates. 1 2 3 4 5 6 7
60. MBEs sometimes act as a "front" for non-minority business. 1 2 3 4 5 6 7
61. MBEs lack qualified engineering personnel. 1 2 3 4 5 6 7
62. MBEs lack qualified managerial personnel. 1 2 3 4 5 6 7
63. MBEs lack qualified sales personnel. 1 2 3 4 5 6 7

Instructions: Below are ways to evaluate aspects of Minority Business Enterprise (MBE) purchasing programs. Read each statement carefully and think about your own firm. Then indicate whether you (1) **Strongly Disagree**, (2) **Moderately Disagree**, (3) **Slightly Disagree**, (4) **Neither Agree nor Disagree**, (5) **Slightly Agree**, (6) **Moderately Agree**, or (7) **Strongly Agree** that each item should be part of **a large company's MBE program** by circling the appropriate number next to the statement.

1	2	3	4	5	6	7
STRONGLY DISAGREE	MODERATELY DISAGREE	SLIGHTLY DISAGREE	NEITHER AGREE NOR DISAGREE	SLIGHTLY AGREE	MODERATELY AGREE	STRONGLY AGREE

This item should be part of a large company's MBE purchasing program.
1. Total sales dollars of MBE purchasing. 1 2 3 4 5 6 7
2. Number of MBEs in purchasing program. 1 2 3 4 5 6 7
3. Reaching the firm's federal quota. 1 2 3 4 5 6 7
4. Helping and developing MBEs. 1 2 3 4 5 6 7
5. Establishing personal relationships with MBE personnel. 1 2 3 4 5 6 7
6. Finding creative ways to use MBEs. 1 2 3 4 5 6 7
7. Adding to the buyer's portfolio of creditable MBEs. 1 2 3 4 5 6 7

Instructions: Below are activities that are sometimes used to implement aspects of Minority Business Enterprise (MBE) purchasing programs. Read each statement carefully and think about your own company. Then indicate whether you (1) **Strongly Disagree**, (2) **Moderately Disagree**, (3) **Slightly Disagree**, (4) **Neither Agree nor Disagree**, (5) **Slightly Agree**, (6) **Moderately Agree**, or (7) **Strongly Agree** that the activity should be part of **a large corporation's MBE program** by circling the appropriate number next to the statement.

1 STRONGLY DISAGREE	2 MODERATELY DISAGREE	3 SLIGHTLY DISAGREE	4 NEITHER AGREE NOR DISAGREE	5 SLIGHTLY AGREE	6 MODERATELY AGREE	7 STRONGLY AGREE

This item should be part of a large company's MBE purchasing program.

1. Provide or use a certification process.	1 2 3 4 5 6 7
2. Offer management assistance.	1 2 3 4 5 6 7
3. Engage in joint ventures.	1 2 3 4 5 6 7
4. Employ company expediters to offer aid to MBEs.	1 2 3 4 5 6 7
5. Give MBEs access to company technical resources.	1 2 3 4 5 6 7
6. Make company internal training available to MBEs.	1 2 3 4 5 6 7
7. Sponsor MBE attendance at business education programs.	1 2 3 4 5 6 7
8. Offer materials management and supply help.	1 2 3 4 5 6 7
9. Hold quality assurance meetings.	1 2 3 4 5 6 7
10. Offer loans or loan guarantees to MBEs.	1 2 3 4 5 6 7
11. Offer subsidies to MBEs.	1 2 3 4 5 6 7
12. Develop national agreements with black/Hispanic groups.	1 2 3 4 5 6 7
13. Attend MBE trade fairs.	1 2 3 4 5 6 7
14. Place ads in the minority press.	1 2 3 4 5 6 7
15. Establish prepayment agreements.	1 2 3 4 5 6 7
16. Hire minority purchasing agents.	1 2 3 4 5 6 7
17. Invest in venture capital pools for MBEs.	1 2 3 4 5 6 7
18. Waive restrictive requirements.	1 2 3 4 5 6 7
19. Employ automated monitoring/tracking of MBE agreements.	1 2 3 4 5 6 7
20. Monitor MBE participation in subcontracts.	1 2 3 4 5 6 7
21. Implement program audits.	1 2 3 4 5 6 7
22. Help with bid preparation.	1 2 3 4 5 6 7
23. Train purchasing agents in problems of MBEs.	1 2 3 4 5 6 7
24. Require performance bonds.	1 2 3 4 5 6 7
25. Perform credit checks.	1 2 3 4 5 6 7
26. Check references.	1 2 3 4 5 6 7
27. Check letters of credit.	1 2 3 4 5 6 7
28. Set specific purchasing target goals for MBEs.	1 2 3 4 5 6 7
29. Establish an MBE advocate program within the company.	1 2 3 4 5 6 7
30. Develop capability to monitor MBE purchases.	1 2 3 4 5 6 7
31. Visibility and commendations for buyer participation in MBE program.	1 2 3 4 5 6 7
32. Get top management involved in MBE purchasing program.	1 2 3 4 5 6 7
33. Organize a permanent in-house task force.	1 2 3 4 5 6 7
34. Offer monetary incentives for buyers who meet or exceed MBE goals.	1 2 3 4 5 6 7
35. Take a leadership role in MBE economic development in the community.	1 2 3 4 5 6 7
36. Challenge non-minority suppliers to become involved.	1 2 3 4 5 6 7
37. Simplify bidding process.	1 2 3 4 5 6 7
38. Have an MBE vendor listing available to all departments.	1 2 3 4 5 6 7
39. Establish an MBE program in every department.	1 2 3 4 5 6 7
40. Employ automated data bases for MBE procurement.	1 2 3 4 5 6 7
41. Disseminate long-term purchasing needs.	1 2 3 4 5 6 7
42. Provide feedback to unsuccessful bidders.	1 2 3 4 5 6 7
43. Publish general information on supply procedures.	1 2 3 4 5 6 7
44. Publish list of buyer names.	1 2 3 4 5 6 7
45. Publish list of commodities sought.	1 2 3 4 5 6 7
46. List large volume opportunities.	1 2 3 4 5 6 7

Instructions: Below are some statements of preference for how a company should be run. Read each statement carefully and think about a large company that you sell to. Then indicate how similar you think YOU are to TOP MANAGEMENT OF THAT LARGE COMPANY on each item by writing in the appropriate number in the blank next to the statement. Then indicate on each line under IMPORTANCE the number from the scale below that represents how important you personally think each item is.

SIMILARITY TO MANAGEMENT OF LARGE FIRM						IMPORTANCE TO YOU				
VERY DISSIMILAR	SOMEWHAT DISSIMILAR	NEITHER SIMILAR NOR DISSIMILAR	SOMEWHAT SIMILAR	VERY SIMILAR		NOT AT ALL IMPORTANT	NOT VERY IMPORTANT	SOMEWHAT IMPORTANT	VERY IMPORTANT	EXTREMELY IMPORTANT
1	2	3	4	5		1	2	3	4	5

	SIMILARITY	IMPORTANCE
1. <u>Professionalism</u> Should behave in a competent, business-like manner.	_____	_____
2. <u>Community involvement</u> Should be concerned and actively involved in the community.	_____	_____
3. <u>Company individuality</u> Should be unique in the industry.	_____	_____
4. <u>Aggressiveness</u> Should be considered a bold and enterprising company. Actively hustling in the marketplace.	_____	_____
5. <u>Ethical behavior</u> Should be concerned with the honesty and integrity of all employees.	_____	_____
6. <u>Creativity</u> Should be imaginative and innovative.	_____	_____
7. <u>Efficiency</u> Should design jobs with minimum waste and expense.	_____	_____
8. <u>Industry leadership</u> Should be considered the best (#1) in the industry.	_____	_____
9. <u>Quality and service</u> Should make a good product and meet customer needs.	_____	_____
10. <u>Support failures</u> Should be willing to support individual or group risk-taking, even when it fails.	_____	_____
11. <u>Company stability</u> Should maintain the existing operation over time.	_____	_____
12. <u>Creating jobs</u> Should contribute to employment in the community by increasing the number of jobs.	_____	_____
13. <u>Profits</u> Should make as much money as a company can.	_____	_____
14. <u>Reduced labor costs</u> Should reduce the cost of employing workers.	_____	_____
15. <u>High morale</u> Should create a good feeling for workers on the job.	_____	_____
16. <u>Product development</u> Should develop new and different products and services.	_____	_____
17. <u>Open communication</u> Should keep everyone informed about what's going on in the firm.	_____	_____
18. <u>Employee development</u> Should expand the skills and abilities of employees.	_____	_____
19. <u>Company independence</u> Should not be tied to any customer or supplier.	_____	_____
20. <u>Employee satisfaction</u> Should create in workers a feeling of happiness with the job and company.	_____	_____

SOME INFORMATION ABOUT YOU:

Years in current position:_____   Sex:_____Male _____Female   Age: _____

Were you born in:____a big city ____a small city ____rural area

Race/national origin:____black ____Hispanic ____white ____Asian ____Native American ____other

Level of education:____less than high school ____high school graduate ____some college
____college graduate ____some graduate school ____graduate degree

Job title:____**Owner** ____**Senior Manager** ____**Junior Manager**
____**Other** (please specify) _____

Percent of sales from minority business purchasing programs _____%

The item number next to the brief verbal description is taken directly from the survey. Items with an "I" prefix refer to an Impediment item, one of the first 63 questions on pages 1 and 2 of the survey form. Items with an "A" prefix refer to Activities that are the 46 questions on page 3 of the survey. Items with an "E" prefix refer to the Criteria for Evaluation, which are the 7 questions in the middle of page 2. "BVI" stands for Business Value Importance and is constructed from the 20 items on page 4, the outside column. "BVS" stands for Business Value Similarity and is constructed from the 20 items on page 4, the inside column.

I. IMPEDIMENT VARIABLES

Small Numbers

I7. Hard to match.
I30. Not available in specialized areas.
I31. Buyers not aware of available MBEs.
I32. MBEs don't expand to meet corporate needs.
I43. MBEs are in too few industry areas.
I44. MBEs are in too few geographic areas.
I52. Resources to develop MBEs are not there.
I54. Identifying and qualifying MBEs is too costly.

Bounded Rationality (Complexity)

I4. Buyers apply regulations inconsistently.
I11. Buyers don't know much about MBEs.
I13. Buyers are inconsistent.
I25. Buyers rely on the "old-boy" network.
I27. No government enforcement.
I33. MBEs naive about corporations.
I36. MBEs can't handle the paperwork.
I40. Buyers lack incentives.
I46. MBEs are poor bidders.
I47. Buyers feel stress and conflict.
I50. Programs are blocked by national agreements.
I51. Programs are blocked by unions.
I53. Buyers lack imagination.
I55. Buyers are out on their own.
I56. High buyer turnover.
I57. Programs are at odds with good purchasing practice.
I58. Programs compromise professional standards.

Business Uncertainty

I34. MBEs not price-competitive.
I45. MBE performance too uncertain.
I62. MBEs lack managerial personnel.
I63. MBEs lack sales personnel.

Production Uncertainty

I24. MBEs need long lead times to correct quality.
I38. MBEs hide problems.
I48. MBEs have inefficient capacities.
I49. Subcontractors impossible to monitor.
I59. MBEs have high failure rates.

Opportunism

I14. Buyers use MBEs for statistics only.
I21. Lack of corporate commitment to MBE program.
I42. MBE programs are all politics.
I60. MBEs are front organizations.

Impacted Information

I2. Looking for contracts is time-consuming.
I3. MBEs have difficulty advertising.
I6. Corporations don't get the word out.
I11. Buyers don't know much about MBEs.
I13. Buyers are inconsistent in implementing the program.
I28. Lead times for quotes too short.
I29. Lead times for deliveries too short.

Atmosphere

I8. Designation "minority business" hurts MBEs.
I18. Hard to get a foot in the door.
I19. MBEs disillusioned with bureaucracy.
I23. Cultural misunderstandings hurt MBEs.
I39. Racial biases hurt programs.

Resource Dependence

I5. It's difficult for MBEs to get information.
I10. MBEs can't compete with bigger firms.
I12. MBEs need technical assistance.
I16. Corporations don't give feedback.
I20. MBEs are undercapitalized.
I22. MBEs are powerless to negotiate.
I26. Only small-volume orders are placed with MBEs.
I34. MBEs are not price-competitive.
I45. MBE performance too uncertain.
I61. MBEs lack engineering personnel.
I62. MBEs lack managerial personnel.
I63. MBEs lack sales personnel.

II. ACTIVITY VARIABLES

Monitoring of MBEs

A9. Hold quality control meetings.
A23. Train buyers in MBE problems.
A24. Require performance bonds.
A25. Perform credit checks.
A26. Check references.
A27. Check letters of credit.

Monitoring of CPPs

A19. Automate tracking of MBEs.
A20. Monitor subcontractors.
A21. Implement program audits.
A28. Set specific target purchasing goals.
A29. Use MBE advocate in corporation.
A30. Develop capability to monitor MBE purchases.
A31. Visibility for buyer participation.
A32. Get top management involved.
A33. Organize an in-house task force.
A34. Offer monetary incentives to buyers.
A39. Have MBE program in each department.

Searching for MBEs

A12. Have national agreements with black/Hispanic groups.
A13. Attend MBE trade fairs.
A14. Place ads in minority press.
A37. Simplify the bidding process.
A38. Have MBE list in each department.
A40. Use automated data bases for MBEs.

Searching for Corporations

A35. Take the lead in minority economic development.
A41. Disseminate long-term purchasing needs.
A43. Publish general information about procedures.
A44. Publish list of buyer names.
A45. Publish lists of commodities sought.
A46. List large-volume opportunities.

Financial Assistance

A10. Offer loans and guarantees.
A11. Offer subsidies.
A15. Establish prepay agreements.

Managerial Assistance

A1. Use certification process.
A2. Offer management assistance.
A7. Sponsor MBEs at business education programs.
A42. Provide feedback on bidding to MBEs.

Technical Assistance

A5. Provide access to technical resources.
A8. Offer materials management and supply help.
A22. Help with bid preparation.

Cultural Interaction

A16. Hire minority buyers.
A23. Train buyers in MBE problems.
A36. Challenge non-minority suppliers.

Internalization

A3. Engage in joint ventures.
A5. Provide MBEs access to technical resources.
A6. Provide MBEs access to internal training.
A17. Invest in venture capital pools for MBEs.

TABLE E1
ACTIVITIES
TOP FIFTEEN
CORPORATE SAMPLE

Item	Mean	Stand Dev.	Rank
Attend MBE Trade Fairs	6.17	1.08	1
MBE List Available to All Departments	5.96	1.26	2
Check References	5.87	1.13	3
Use Certification Process	5.83	1.30	4
Get Top Management Involved	5.72	1.47	5
Check Letters of Credit	5.71	1.24	6
Develop Capability to Monitor	5.71	1.19	7
Perform Credit Checks	5.69	1.24	8
Hold Quality Control Meetings	5.61	1.29	9
Publish List of Commodities Sought	5.55	1.39	10
Publish General Information on Procedures	5.49	1.33	11
Provide Feedback	5.48	1.50	12
Train Buyers in MBE Problems	5.46	1.36	13
Use MBE Advocate in Corporation	5.39	1.38	14
Place Ads in Minority Press	5.32	1.48	15

TABLE E2
ACTIVITIES
BOTTOM FIFTEEN
CORPORATE SAMPLE

Item	Mean	Stand Dev.	Rank
Offer Subsidies	2.68	1.60	1
Waive Restrictive Requirements	2.76	1.70	2
Offer Loans and Guarantees	3.15	1.79	3
Offer Monetary Incentives to Buyers	3.21	2.01	4
Establish Prepay Agreements	3.62	1.75	5
Invest in Venture Capital Pools for MBEs	3.77	1.65	6
Help with Bid Preparation	3.89	1.86	7
MBE Access to Tech Resources	3.91	1.73	8
Use Company Expediters	4.00	1.70	9
MBE Access to Internal Training	4.03	1.75	10
Simplify Bidding Process	4.11	1.85	11
Require Performance Bonds	4.23	1.41	12
Offer Materials Mgmt. and Supply Help	4.34	1.68	13
Nat'l Agreements w/ blacks and Hispanics	4.43	1.76	14
Organize In-House Task Force	4.63	1.67	15

TABLE E3
EVALUATIONS
CORPORATE SAMPLE

Item	Mean	Stand Dev.	Rank
Increasing Buyers' Portfolio	5.81	1.28	1
Creative Uses of MBEs	5.64	1.38	2
Helping and Developing MBEs	5.63	1.44	3
Total Sales Dollars	5.26	1.77	4
Number of MBEs in Program	5.14	1.74	5
Establish Personal Relationships	4.83	1.77	6
Firms' Federal Quota	4.65	1.82	7

TABLE E4
IMPEDIMENTS
TOP FIFTEEN
CORPORATE SAMPLE

Item	Mean	Stand Dev.	Rank
Powerless to Negotiate	5.08	1.55	1
Disillusioned with Bureaucracy	5.07	1.35	2
Not Available in Specialized Areas	4.94	1.70	3
Difficult to Get Information	4.76	1.86	4
MBEs are Front Organizations	4.72	1.41	5
MBEs are in too few Industry Areas	4.52	1.50	6
Time-Consuming	4.46	1.65	7
Buyers Need MBEs for Statistics	4.44	1.85	8
MBEs Don't Expand to Meet Corporate Needs	4.42	1.35	9
Buyers Feel Stress and Conflict	4.41	1.69	10
High Buyer Turnover	4.40	1.72	11
ID and Qualifying MBEs Too Costly	4.40	1.62	12
Buyers Lack Information	4.38	1.63	13
Hard to Match	4.35	1.80	14
Buyers Not Aware of Available MBEs	4.31	1.82	15

TABLE E5
IMPEDIMENTS
BOTTOM FIFTEEN
CORPORATE SAMPLE

Item	Mean	Stand Dev.	Rank
Not Very Profitable	2.50	1.68	1
MBEs Undercapitalized	2.68	1.31	2
MBEs Need Technical Assistance	2.93	1.45	3
Lack of Corp. Commit. to MBE Purch. Prgrms.	2.93	1.91	4
Lead Times for Quotes Too Short	3.02	1.35	5
Designation MBE Hurts	3.02	1.81	6
Lead Times for Deliveries too Short	3.04	1.39	7
Compromise Professional Standards	3.09	1.78	8
Lack of Imagination	3.11	1.77	9
Buyers Lack Incentives	3.18	1.89	10
MBEs Can't Meet Bid Deadlines	3.19	1.46	11
Don't Get Word Out	3.27	1.86	12
Resources to Develop MBEs Not There	3.28	1.72	13
Blocked by Unions	3.37	1.35	14
Apply Regs. Inconsistently	3.47	1.97	15

TABLE E6
ACTIVITIES
TOP FIFTEEN
SMALL BUSINESS SAMPLE

Item	Mean	Stand Dev.	Rank
Provide Feedback	5.80	1.24	1
Check References	5.78	1.23	2
List Large-Volume Opportunities	5.74	1.23	3
Publish List of Buyer Names	5.69	1.33	4
Publish General Information on Procedures	5.69	1.20	5
Publish List of Commodities Sought	5.69	1.13	6
Hire Minority Buyers	5.60	1.33	7
MBE List Available to All Depts.	5.53	1.29	8
Simplify Bidding Process	5.50	1.30	9
Attend MBE Trade Fairs	5.34	1.37	10
Train Buyers in MBE Problems	5.30	1.20	11
Check Letters of Credit	5.29	1.36	12
Hold Quality Control Meetings	5.29	1.17	13
Perform Credit Checks	5.23	1.35	14
Get Top Management Involved	5.13	1.31	15

TABLE E7
ACTIVITIES
BOTTOM FIFTEEN
SMALL BUSINESS SAMPLE

Item	Mean	Stand Dev.	Rank
Offer Subsidies	2.97	1.56	1
Offer Monetary Incentives to Buyers	3.70	1.58	2
Offer Loans and Guarantees	3.71	1.77	3
Waive Restrictive Requirements	3.76	1.63	4
Require Performance Bonds	3.76	1.64	5
Nat'l Agreements w/ blacks and Hispanics	4.04	1.71	6
Use Company Expediters	4.08	1.43	7
Invest in Venture Capital Pools for MBEs	4.13	1.48	8
Organize In-House Task Force	4.20	1.24	9
Automate Tracking of MBEs	4.33	1.25	10
Offer Management Assistance	4.45	1.48	11
Help with Bid Preparation	4.46	1.53	12
Offer Mat'ls Mgmt. and Supply Help	4.57	1.45	13
Implement Program Audits	4.58	1.28	14
MBE Access to Internal Training	4.60	1.49	15

TABLE E8
EVALUATIONS
SMALL BUSINESS SAMPLE

Item	Mean	Stand Dev.	Rank
Increasing Buyers' Portfolio	5.45	1.24	1
Creative Uses of MBEs	5.16	1.51	2
Establish Personal Relationships	5.08	1.44	3
Helping and Developing MBEs	4.99	1.30	4
Number of MBEs in Program	4.56	1.37	5
Total Sales Dollars	4.51	1.51	6
Firms' Federal Quota	4.25	1.58	7

TABLE E9
IMPEDIMENTS
TOP FIFTEEN
SMALL BUSINESS SAMPLE

Item	Mean	Stand Dev.	Rank
MBEs Not Price-Competitive	5.47	1.48	1
Don't Get Word Out	5.11	1.55	2
Disillusioned with Bureaucracy	5.07	1.50	3
Hard to Get Foot in Door	5.04	1.63	4
MBE Performance Too Uncertain	4.98	1.54	5
MBEs Lack Sales Personnel	4.88	1.59	6
MBEs Lack Managerial Personnel	4.85	1.73	7
Rely on "Old-Boy" Networks	4.83	1.42	8
Buyers Not Aware of Available MBEs	4.77	1.41	9
Buyers Lack Information	4.75	1.63	10
Lack of Corp. Commit. to MBE Purch. Prgrms.	4.75	1.29	11
MBEs Can't Compete	4.73	1.95	12
Time-Consuming	4.63	1.86	13
Too Long to Pay	4.60	1.78	14
Buyers are Inconsistent	4.60	1.26	15

TABLE E10
IMPEDIMENTS
BOTTOM FIFTEEN
SMALL BUSINESS SAMPLE

Item	Mean	Stand Dev.	Rank
MBEs Can't Meet Bid Deadlines	2.58	1.50	1
Long Lead Times to Correct Quality	2.59	1.41	2
MBEs Undercapitalized	2.73	1.47	3
Not Very Profitable	2.90	1.77	4
MBEs Have Inefficient Capacities	2.95	1.52	5
MBEs Hide Problems	3.11	1.67	6
MBEs Can't Handle Paperwork	3.16	1.78	7
MBEs Have "Give-Me" Attitude	3.17	1.64	8
Subcontractors Impossible to Monitor	3.18	1.60	9
MBEs Poor Bidders	3.18	1.61	10
Compromise Professional Standards	3.21	1.58	11
MBEs Naive About Corporations	3.24	1.71	12
Not Available in Specialized Areas	3.31	1.43	13
MBEs Need Technical Assistance	3.34	1.59	14
Corporations Don't Give Feedback	3.42	1.55	15

TABLE E11
ACTIVITIES
TOP FIFTEEN
MINORITY BUSINESS SAMPLE

Item	Mean	Stand Dev.	Rank
Publish List of Commodities Sought	6.52	.87	1
MBE List Available to All Departments	6.44	1.00	2
List Large-Volume Opportunities	6.42	.98	3
Provide Feedback	6.31	1.09	4
Get Top Management Involved	6.31	1.08	5
Publish List of Buyer Names	6.31	1.04	6
Publish General Information on Procedures	6.23	1.00	7
Set Specific Target Purchasing Goals	6.21	1.10	8
Develop Capability to Monitor	6.20	1.12	9
Use MBE Advocate in Corporation	6.00	1.23	10
Visibility for Buyer Participation	5.99	1.26	11
Monitor Subcontractors	5.96	1.28	12
Attend MBE Trade Fairs	5.95	1.36	13
Lead in Economic Development	5.94	1.27	14
Disseminate List of Purch. Needs	5.92	1.27	15

TABLE E12
ACTIVITIES
BOTTOM FIFTEEN
MINORITY BUSINESS SAMPLE

Item	Mean	Stand Dev.	Rank
Require Performance Bonds	3.79	1.78	1
Offer Subsidies	4.18	1.89	2
Waive Restrictive Requirements	4.42	1.95	3
Help with Bid Preparation	4.71	1.76	4
Offer Mat'ls Mgmt. and Supply Help	4.91	1.49	5
Use Company Expediters	4.92	1.72	6
Perform Credit Checks	4.94	1.72	7
MBE Access to Internal Training	4.97	1.59	8
Offer Loans and Guarantees	5.03	1.85	9
Nat'l Agreement w/ blacks & Hispanics	5.07	1.86	10
Offer Management Assistance	5.08	1.63	11
Offer Monetary Incentives to Buyers	5.10	1.87	12
Establish Prepay Agreements	5.23	1.69	13
MBE Attends Business Ed Programs	5.31	1.50	14
Check Letters of Credit	5.31	1.60	15

TABLE E13
EVALUATIONS
MINORITY BUSINESS SAMPLE

Item	Mean	Stand Dev.	Rank
Increasing Buyers' Portfolio	6.37	1.08	1
Creative Uses of MBEs	6.23	1.13	2
Helping and Developing MBEs	5.93	1.44	3
Establish Personal Relationships	5.74	1.55	4
Firms' Federal Quota	5.68	1.64	5
Total Sales Dollars	5.63	1.70	6
Number of MBEs in Program	5.57	1.59	7

TABLE E14
IMPEDIMENTS
TOP FIFTEEN
MINORITY BUSINESS SAMPLE

Item	Mean	Stand Dev.	Rank
Rely on "Old-Boy" Networks	6.26	1.11	1
Buyers Need MBEs for Statistics	6.17	1.13	2
Hard to Get Foot in Door	6.01	1.40	3
Buyers are Inconsistent	5.95	1.30	4
No Government Enforcement	5.91	1.61	5
Lack of Corp. Commit. to MBE Purch. Prgrms.	5.91	1.42	6
Buyers Don't Know Much	5.91	1.33	7
Buyers Don't Work Closely	5.78	1.41	8
Disillusioned with Bureaucracy	5.74	1.40	9
Buyers Lack Incentives	5.65	1.48	10
Don't Get Word Out	5.60	1.66	11
Buyers Lack Information	5.56	1.67	12
Apply Regs. Inconsistently	5.48	1.60	13
Buyers Not Aware of Available MBEs	5.47	1.63	14
Racial Biases Hurt Programs	5.38	1.77	15

TABLE E15
IMPEDIMENTS
BOTTOM FIFTEEN
MINORITY BUSINESS SAMPLE

Item	Mean	Stand Dev.	Rank
MBEs Undercapitalized	2.08	1.41	1
Only Small-Volume Orders	2.11	1.43	2
Corporations Don't Give Feedback	2.18	1.37	3
Difficult to Get Information	2.77	1.73	4
MBEs Can't Meet Bid Deadlines	2.85	1.96	5
MBEs Can't Compete	2.90	2.22	6
MBEs Have "Give-Me" Attitude	3.08	1.98	7
MBEs Can't Handle Paperwork	3.10	2.13	8
MBEs Need Technical Assistance	3.19	1.71	9
Powerless to Negotiate	3.24	1.80	10
MBEs Poor Bidders	3.27	1.66	11
Not Very Profitable	3.30	2.15	12
MBEs Have Inefficient Capacities	3.31	1.82	13
Long Lead Times to Correct Quality	3.40	1.97	14
MBEs Hide Problems	3.59	1.97	15

TABLE E16
ACTIVITIES
TOP FIFTEEN
TOTAL SAMPLE

Item	Mean	Stand Dev.	Rank
Attend MBE Trade Fairs	6.04	1.19	1
MBE List Available to All Departments	5.98	1.24	2
Check References	5.85	1.16	3
Get Top Management Involved	5.75	1.43	4
Publish List of Commodities Sought	5.74	1.35	5
Use Certification Process	5.73	1.39	6
Develop Capability to Monitor	5.71	1.21	7
Provide Feedback	5.64	1.44	8
Publish General Information on Procedures	5.62	1.30	9
Check Letters of Credit	5.61	1.32	10
Hold Quality Control Meetings	5.58	1.29	11
Perform Credit Checks	5.52	1.37	12
Train Buyers in MBE Problems	5.51	1.35	13
Use MBE Advocate in Corporation	5.42	1.37	14
List Large-Volume Opportunities	5.40	1.50	15

TABLE E17
ACTIVITIES
BOTTOM FIFTEEN
TOTAL SAMPLE

Item	Mean	Stand Dev.	Rank
Offer Subsidies	2.94	1.73	1
Waive Restrictive Requirements	3.12	1.84	2
Offer Loans and Guarantees	3.50	1.91	3
Offer Monetary Incentives to Buyers	3.55	2.05	4
Establish Prepay Agreements	3.99	1.83	5
Invest in Venture Capital Pools for MBEs	4.05	1.71	6
Help with Bid Preparation	4.08	1.84	7
Require Performance Bonds	4.12	1.51	8
Use Company Expediters	4.15	1.71	9
MBE Access to Internal Training	4.24	1.73	10
MBE Access to Tech Resources	4.24	1.75	11
Offer Mat'ls Mgmt. and Supply Help	4.45	1.64	12
Nat'l Agreements w/ blacks & Hispanics	4.48	1.79	13
Simplify Bidding Process	4.50	1.87	14
Organize In-House Task Force	4.70	1.64	15

TABLE E18
EVALUATIONS
TOTAL SAMPLE

Item	Mean	Stand Dev.	Rank
Increasing Buyers' Portfolio	5.85	1.27	1
Creative Uses of MBEs	5.68	1.38	2
Helping and Developing MBEs	5.61	1.44	3
Total Sales Dollars	5.23	1.76	4
Number of MBEs in Program	5.13	1.70	5
Establish Personal Relationships	4.99	1.74	6
Firms' Federal Quota	4.76	1.81	7

TABLE E19
IMPEDIMENTS
TOP FIFTEEN
TOTAL SAMPLE

Item	Mean	Stand Dev.	Rank
Disillusioned with Bureaucracy	5.15	1.40	1
Buyers Need MBEs for Statistics	4.68	1.84	2
Powerless to Negotiate	4.68	1.75	3
MBEs are Front Organizations	4.62	1.49	4
Time-Consuming	4.61	1.74	5
Buyers Lack Information	4.60	1.69	6
Not Available in Specialized Areas	4.59	1.81	7
Hard to Get Foot in Door	4.55	1.94	8
Buyers Not Aware of Available MBEs	4.54	1.80	9
MBEs Are in Too Few Industry Areas	4.42	1.55	10
Buyers Don't Know Much	4.38	1.88	11
Buyers Are Inconsistent	4.38	1.78	12
Difficulty Advertising	4.35	1.76	13
Buyers Feel Stress and Conflict	4.35	1.67	14
MBE Performance Too Uncertain	4.35	1.59	15

TABLE E20
IMPEDIMENTS
BOTTOM FIFTEEN
TOTAL SAMPLE

Item	Mean	Stand Dev.	Rank
MBEs Undercapitalized	2.58	1.36	1
Not Very Profitable	2.67	1.80	2
MBEs Need Technical Assistance	3.02	1.52	3
Compromise Professional Standards	3.06	1.77	4
MBEs Can't Meet Bid Deadlines	3.07	1.57	5
Lead Times for Deliveries Too Short	3.30	1.50	6
MBE Designation Hurts	3.35	1.90	7
Lead Times for Quotes Too Short	3.37	1.57	8
MBEs Can't Handle Paperwork	3.41	1.63	9
Long Lead Times to Correct Quality	3.44	1.59	10
Lack of Imagination	3.51	1.84	11
MBEs Poor Bidders	3.59	1.48	12
Resources to Develop MBEs Not There	3.59	1.74	13
Lack of Corp. Commit. to MBE Purch. Prgrms.	3.62	2.12	14
MBEs Have Inefficient Capacities	3.65	1.46	15

TABLE F1
ONE-WAY ANALYSIS OF VARIANCE OF IMPEDIMENT
SCALES BY GROUP MEMBERSHIP

	MBE	SBE	CPP	Differences		
Scale	Mean (1)	Mean (2)	Mean (3)	1-2	1-3	2-3
Small Numbers	35.01	31.09	34.12	*		*
Bounded Rationality	80.65	68.61	62.89	*	*	*
Business Uncertainty	13.54	12.02	15.96		*	*
Production Uncertainty	18.21	15.58	19.43	*	*	*
Opportunism	21.98	16.64	16.13	*	*	
Atmosphere	32.16	25.93	23.11	*	*	*
Impacted Information	36.26	30.88	26.04	*	*	*
Resource Dependence	41.73	50.45	47.83	*	*	
Value Similarity	81.58	74.33	78.20	*	*	*
Value Importance	84.59	81.70	83.40			

* denotes significant difference at 0.05 probability level.

Table F1 indicates that the MBEs differ from their corporate counterparts on all transaction cost variables except small numbers (column marked "1-3"). The MBEs also differed from the SBEs on all variables except business uncertainty (column "1-2") and the SBEs differed from the corporate responses on all variables except opportunism and resource dependence (column "2-3"). The table indicates that MBEs face the most complexity, opportunism, impacted information, and problems of atmosphere. CPPs feel the problems of production uncertainty the most.

TABLE F2
ANALYSIS OF VARIANCE OF THE IMPEDIMENT SCALES
MAIN EFFECTS OF GROUP, RACE, AND EDUCATION

SMALL NUMBERS

Source of Variation	Sum of Squares	DF	Mean Square	F	Sig. of F
Main Effects	1706.440	12	142.203	2.586	.002
Group	780.880	2	390.440	7.100	.001
Race	214.801	5	42.960	.781	.563
Education	386.354	5	77.271	1.405	.220
Explained	1706.440	12	142.203	2.586	.002
Residual	53283.067	969	54.988		
Total	54989.507	981	56.055		

BUSINESS UNCERTAINTY

Source of Variation	Sum of Squares	DF	Mean Square	F	Sig. of F
Main Effects	2392.381	12	199.365	8.268	.000
Group	1547.233	2	773.616	32.085	.000
Race	424.391	5	84.878	3.520	.004
Education	22.650	5	4.530	.188	.967
Explained	2392.381	12	199.365	8.268	.000
Residual	22954.289	952	24.112		
Total	25346.669	964	26.293		

PRODUCTION UNCERTAINTY

Source of Variation	Sum of Squares	DF	Mean Square	F	Sig. of F
Main Effects	1821.991	12	151.833	6.091	.000
Group	1414.848	2	707.424	28.381	.000
Race	199.354	5	39.871	1.600	.157
Education	113.155	5	151.833	.908	.475
Explained	1821.991	12	151.833	6.091	.000
Residual	23903.671	959	24.926		
Total	25725.663	971	26.494		

BOUNDED RATIONALITY

Source of Variation	Sum of Squares	DF	Mean Square	F	Sig. of F
Main Effects	45754.293	12	3812.858	18.576	.000
Group	10702.365	2	5351.183	26.071	.000
Race	5191.148	5	1038.230	5.058	.000
Education	1200.575	5	240.115	1.170	.322
Explained	45754.293	12	3812.858	18.576	.000
Residual	193145.744	941	205.256		
Total	238900.038	953	250.682		

TABLE F2 continued

OPPORTUNISM

Source of Variation	Sum of Squares	DF	Mean Square	F	Sig. of F
Main Effects	5257.766	12	438.147	24.684	.000
Group	889.555	2	444.778	25.058	.000
Race	624.857	5	124.971	7.041	.000
Education	67.693	5	13.539	.763	.577
Explained	5257.766	12	438.147	24.684	.000
Residual	17128.669	965	17.750		
Total	22386.435	977	22.913		

IMPACTED INFORMATION

Source of Variation	Sum of Squares	DF	Mean Square	F	Sig. of F
Main Effects	16661.613	12	1388.468	29.707	.000
Group	4870.754	2	2435.377	52.107	.000
Race	2064.798	5	412.960	8.836	.000
Education	272.723	5	54.545	1.167	.323
Explained	16661.613	12	1388.468	29.707	.000
Residual	45009.009	963	46.738		
Total	61670.622	975	63.252		

ATMOSPHERE

Source of Variation	Sum of Squares	DF	Mean Square	F	Sig. of F
Main Effects	15730.148	12	1310.846	34.932	.000
Group	1800.679	2	900.340	23.992	.000
Race	4846.086	5	969.217	25.828	.000
Education	371.011	5	74.202	1.977	.080
Explained	15370.148	12	1310.846	34.932	.000
Residual	35912.418	957	37.526		
Total	51642.566	969	53.295		

RESOURCE DEPENDENCE

Source of Variation	Sum of Squares	DF	Mean Square	F	Sig. of F
Main Effects	7566.325	12	630.527	5.895	.000
Group	1443.417	2	721.708	6.747	.001
Race	1411.022	5	282.204	2.638	.022
Education	382.506	5	76.501	.715	.612
Explained	7566.325	12	630.527	5.895	.000
Residual	102582.971	959	106.969		
Total	110149.296	971	113.439		

(VALUE SIMILARITY/VALUE IMPORTANCE---No Significant Main Effects)

TABLE F3
ONE-WAY ANALYSIS OF VARIANCE OF ACTIVITIES
SCALES BY GROUP MEMBERSHIP

Scale	MBE Mean (1)	SBE Mean (2)	CPP Mean (3)	Differences 1-2	1-3	2-3
Monitoring of MBEs	36.11	34.63	36.57			*
Monitoring of CPPs	64.18	50.69	55.03	*	*	*
Searching for MBEs	34.73	29.85	30.85	*	*	
Searching for CPPs	37.32	33.23	31.33	*	*	*
Financial Assistance	14.76	11.78	9.47	*	*	*
Managerial Assistance	22.43	19.98	21.24	*	*	*
Technical Assistance	15.22	14.14	12.42		*	*
Cultural Interaction	16.93	15.22	15.30	*	*	
Internalization	21.39	18.53	16.58	*	*	*

* Denotes significant difference at 0.05 probability level.

TABLE F4
ANALYSIS OF VARIANCE OF ACTIVITY SCALES
MAIN EFFECTS OF GROUP, RACE, AND EDUCATION

MONITORING OF MBEs

Source of Variation	Sum of Squares	DF	Mean Square	F	Sig. of F
Main Effects	936.251	12	78.021	2.672	.002
Group	381.202	2	190.601	6.528	.002
Race	326.134	5	65.227	2.234	.049
Education	246.496	5	49.299	1.688	.135
Explained	936.251	12	78.021	2.672	.002
Residual	28089.868	962	29.199		
Total	29026.119	974	29.801		

MONITORING OF CORPORATIONS

Source of Variation	Sum of Squares	DF	Mean Square	F	Sig. of F
Main Effects	18963.686	12	1580.307	14.932	.000
Group	2034.014	2	1017.007	9.610	.000
Race	4974.655	5	994.931	9.401	.000
Education	569.369	5	113.874	1.076	.372
Explained	18963.445	12	1580.307	14.932	.000
Residual	100962.445	954	105.831		
Total	119926.130	966	124.147	

SEARCHING FOR MBEs

Source of Variation	Sum of Squares	DF	Mean Square	F	Sig. of F
Main Effects	3742.233	12	311.853	11.815	.000
Group	124.785	2	62.692	2.364	.095
Race	1547.520	5	309.504	11.726	.000
Education	111.124	5	22.225	.842	.520
Explained	3742.233	12	311.853	11.815	.000
Residual	25392.102	962	26.395		
Total	29134.334	974	29.912		

SEARCHING FOR CORPORATIONS

Source of Variation	Sum of Squares	DF	Mean Square	F	Sig. of F
Main Effects	5866.562	12	488.880	14.660	.000
Group	1040.853	2	520.427	15.606	.000
Race	953.929	5	190.786	5.721	.000
Education	503.450	5	100.690	3.019	.010
Explained	5866.562	12	488.880	14.660	.000
Residual	31746.686	952	33.347		
Total	37613.248	964	39.018		

FINANCIAL ASSISTANCE

Source of Variation	Sum of Squares	DF	Mean Square	F	Sig. of F
Main Effects	3905.383	12	325.449	17.702	.000
Group	970.032	2	485.016	26.381	.000
Race	521.372	5	104.274	5.672	.000
Education	23.950	5	4.790	.261	.935
Explained	3905.383	12	325.449	17.702	.000
Residual	16252.513	884	18.385		
Total	20157.895	896	22.498		

MANAGERIAL ASSISTANCE

Source of Variation	Sum of Squares	DF	Mean Square	F	Sig. of F
Main Effects	913.205	12	76.100	5.187	.000
Group	137.197	2	68.598	4.676	.010
Race	450.041	5	90.008	6.135	.000
Education	101.393	5	20.279	1.382	.228
Explained	913.205	12	76.100	5.187	.000
Residual	14127.873	963	14.671		
Total	15041.078	975	15.267		

TECHNICAL ASSISTANCE

Source of Variation	Sum of Squares	DF	Mean Square	F	Sig. of F
Main Effects	1479.464	12	123.289	7.311	.000
Group	342.763	2	171.382	10.163	.000
Race	362.580	5	72.516	4.300	.001
Education	55.537	5	11.107	.659	.655
Explained	1479.464	12	123.289	7.311	.000
Residual	15143.691	898	16.864		
Total	16623.155	910	18.267		

CULTURAL INTERACTION

Source of Variation	Sum of Squares	DF	Mean Square	F	Sig. of F
Main Effects	1037.258	12	86.438	8.660	.000
Group	.294	2	.147	.015	.985
Race	646.373	5	129.275	12.952	.000
Education	38.985	5	7.797	.781	.563
Explained	1037.258	12	86.438	8.660	.000
Residual	9531.949	955	9.981		
Total	10569.207	967	10.930		

INTERNALIZATION

Source of Variation	Sum of Squares	DF	Mean Square	F	Sig. of F
Main Effects	3828.828	12	319.069	14.021	.000
Group	747.520	2	373.760	16.424	.000
Race	804.222	5	160.844	7.068	.000
Education	73.394	5	14.679	.645	.665
Explained	3828.828	12	319.069	14.021	.000
Residual	21550.496	947	22.757		
Total	25379.324	959	26.464		

TABLE F5
ONE-WAY ANALYSIS OF VARIANCE ON CRITERIA FOR
EVALUATING MBE PURCHASING PROGRAMS BY GROUP

Scale	MBE Mean (1)	SBE Mean (2)	CPP Mean (3)	Differences 1-2	1-3	2-3
Total Sales Dollars	5.63	4.51	5.26	*		*
Number of MBEs in Program	5.57	4.55	5.14	*	*	*
Federal Quota	5.67	4.25	4.65	*	*	
Helping and Developing MBEs	5.93	4.99	5.63	*		*
Establishing Personal Relationships	5.74	5.08	4.99	*	*	
Creative uses of MBEs	6.23	5.15	5.63	*	*	*
Increasing Buyers' Portfolios	6.37	5.45	5.81	*	*	*

* denotes significance at 0.05 probability level.

TABLE F6
ANALYSIS OF VARIANCE OF CRITERIA FOR EVALUATING MBE
PURCHASING PROGRAMS BY GROUP, RACE, AND EDUCATION

TOTAL SALES DOLLARS

Source of Variation	Sum of Squares	DF	Mean Square	F	Sig. of F
Main Effects	139.121	12	11.593	3.902	.000
Group	45.042	2	22.521	7.580	.001
Race	42.095	5	8.419	2.834	.015
Education	16.719	5	3.344	1.125	.345
Explained	139.121	12	11.593	3.902	.000
Residual	2840.286	956	2.971		
Total	2979.408	968	3.078		

NUMBER OF MBEs IN PROGRAM

Source of Variation	Sum of Squares	DF	Mean Square	F	Sig. of F
Main Effects	118.020	12	9.835	3.484	.000
Group	27.074	2	13.537	4.795	.008
Race	41.565	5	8.313	2.944	.012
Education	10.542	5	2.108	.747	.589
Explained	118.020	12	9.835	3.484	.000
Residual	2699.072	956	2.823		
Total	2817.092	968	2.910		

FIRMS' FEDERAL QUOTA

Source of Variation	Sum of Squares	DF	Mean Square	F	Sig. of F
Main Effects	185.066	12	15.422	4.869	.000
Group	57.101	2	28.551	9.014	.000
Race	14.392	5	2.878	.909	.475
Education	7.433	5	1.487	.469	.799
Explained	185.066	12	15.422	4.869	.000
Residual	3028.073	956	3.167		
Total	3213.139	968	3.319		

HELPING AND DEVELOPING MBEs

Source of Variation	Sum of Squares	DF	Mean Square	F	Sig. of F
Main Effects	94.684	12	7.890	3.975	.000
Group	27.739	2	13.869	6.988	.001
Race	28.775	5	5.755	2.900	.013
Education	14.347	5	2.869	1.446	.205
Explained	94.684	12	7.890	3.975	.000
Residual	1897.417	956	1.985		
Total	1992.101	968	2.058		

ESTABLISHING PERSONAL RELATIONSHIPS

Source of Variation	Sum of Squares	DF	Mean Square	F	Sig. of F
Main Effects	110.584	12	9.215	3.147	.000
Group	36.858	2	18.429	6.294	.002
Race	5.310	5	1.062	.363	.874
Education	6.848	5	1.370	.468	.800
Explained	110.584	12	9.215	3.147	.000
Residual	2828.391	966	2.928		
Total	2938.974	978	3.005		

CREATIVE USES OF MBEs

Source of Variation	Sum of Squares	DF	Mean Square	F	Sig. of F
Main Effects	119.279	12	9.940	5.529	.000
Group	19.342	2	9.671	5.580	.005
Race	36.241	5	7.248	4.032	.001
Education	7.433	5	1.487	.827	.531
Explained	119.279	12	9.940	5.529	.000
Residual	1736.559	966	1.798		
Total	1855.839	978	1.898		

INCREASING BUYERS' PORTFOLIOS

Source of Variation	Sum of Squares	DF	Mean Square	F	Sig. of F
Main Effects	102.718	12	8.560	5.693	.000
Group	9.411	2	4.706	3.130	.044
Race	32.463	5	6.493	4.318	.001
Education	13.316	5	2.663	1.771	.116
Explained	102.718	12	8.560	5.693	.000
Residual	1452.390	966	1.504		
Total	1555.107	978	1.590		

TABLE F7
ANALYSIS OF VARIANCE OF IMPEDIMENTS SCALES
BY INDUSTRY GROUP (2-digit SIC)

SMALL NUMBERS

Source of Variation	Sum of Squares	DF	Mean Square	F	Sig. of F
Main Effects	1175.837	7	167.977	3.049	.004
Industry Type	1175.837	7	167.977	3.049	.004
Explained	1175.837	7	167.977	3.049	.004
Residual	37742.079	685	55.098		
Total	38917.916	692	56.240		

BUSINESS UNCERTAINTY

Source of Variation	Sum of Squares	DF	Mean Square	F	Sig. of F
Main Effects	555.119	7	79.303	3.460	.001
Industry Type	555.119	7	79.303	3.460	.001
Explained	555.119	7	79.303	3.460	.001
Residual	15587.158	680	22.922		
Total	16142.278	687	23.497		

PRODUCTION UNCERTAINTY

Source of Variation	Sum of Squares	DF	Mean Square	F	Sig. of F
Main Effects	214.040	7	30.577	1.369	.001
Industry Type	214.040	7	30.577	1.369	.001
Explained	214.040	7	30.577	1.369	.001
Residual	15117.107	677	22.330		
Total	15331.147	684	22.414		

COMPLEXITY

Source of Variation	Sum of Squares	DF	Mean Square	F	Sig. of F
Main Effects	2358.108	7	336.873	1.446	.184
Industry Type	2358.108	7	336.873	1.446	.184
Explained	2358.108	7	336.873	1.446	.184
Residual	154507.689	663	233.043		
Total	156865.797	670	234.128		

OPPORTUNISM

Source of Variation	Sum of Squares	DF	Mean Square	F	Sig. of F
Main Effects	245.962	7	35.137	1.709	.104
Industry Type	245.962	7	35.137	1.709	.104
Explained	245.962	7	35.137	1.709	.104
Residual	13874.689	663	20.555		
Total	14120.489	682	20.705		

IMPACTED INFORMATION

Source of Variation	Sum of Squares	DF	Mean Square	F	Sig. of F
Main Effects	1465.333	7	209.333	4.332	.000
Industry Type	1465.333	7	209.333	4.332	.000
Explained	1465.333	7	209.333	4.332	.000
Residual	32616.380	675	48.321		
Total	34081.713	682	49.973		

ATMOSPHERE

Source of Variation	Sum of Squares	DF	Mean Square	F	Sig. of F
Main Effects	371.708	7	53.101	1.119	.349
Industry Type	371.708	7	53.101	1.119	.349
Explained	371.708	7	53.101	1.119	.349
Residual	31968.569	674	47.458		
Total	32358.277	681	47.516		

RESOURCE DEPENDENCE

Source of Variation	Sum of Squares	DF	Mean Square	F	Sig. of F
Main Effects	1086.053	7	155.150	1.397	.204
Industry Type	1086.053	7	155.150	1.397	.204
Explained	1086.053	7	155.150	1.397	.204
Residual	75211.442	677	111.095		
Total	76297.495	684	111.546		

VALUE SIMILARITY

Source of Variation	Sum of Squares	DF	Mean Square	F	Sig. of F
Main Effects	4453.413	7	636.202	3.292	.002
Industry Type	4453.413	7	636.202	3.292	.002
Explained	4453.413	7	636.202	3.292	.002
Residual	131607.675	681	193.256		
Total	136061.087	688	197.763		

VALUE IMPORTANCE

Source of Variation	Sum of Squares	DF	Mean Square	F	Sig. of F
Main Effects	943.838	7	134.834	.974	.449
Industry Type	943.838	7	134.834	.974	.449
Explained	943.838	7	134.834	.974	.449
Residual	95484.306	690	138.383		
Total	96428.144	697	138.347		

TABLE F8
ANALYSIS OF VARIANCE OF ACTIVITY SCALES
BY INDUSTRY GROUP (2-digit SIC)

MONITORING OF MBEs

Source of Variation	Sum of Squares	DF	Mean Square	F	Sig. of F
Main Effects	273.993	7	39.142	1.340	.228
Industry Type	273.993	7	39.142	1.340	.228
Explained	273.993	7	39.142	1.340	.228
Residual	20121.287	689	29.204		
Total	20395.280	696	29.304		

MONITORING OF CORPORATIONS

Source of Variation	Sum of Squares	DF	Mean Square	F	Sig. of F
Main Effects	3625.393	7	517.913	4.700	.000
Industry Type	3625.393	7	517.913	4.700	.000
Explained	3625.393	7	517.913	4.700	.000
Residual	74824.758	679	110.198		
Total	78450.151	686	114.359		

SEARCHING FOR MBEs

Source of Variation	Sum of Squares	DF	Mean Square	F	Sig. of F
Main Effects	649.567	7	92.795	3.451	.001
Industry Type	649.567	7	92.795	3.451	.001
Explained	649.567	7	92.795	3.451	.001
Residual	18471.766	687	26.888		
Total	19121.332	694	27.552		

SEARCHING FOR CORPORATIONS

Source of Variation	Sum of Squares	DF	Mean Square	F	Sig. of F
Main Effects	456.998	7	65.285	1.710	.104
Industry Type	456.998	7	65.285	1.710	.104
Explained	456.998	7	65.285	1.710	.104
Residual	25959.321	680	38.175		
Total	26416.320	687	38.452		

FINANCIAL ASSISTANCE

Source of Variation	Sum of Squares	DF	Mean Square	F	Sig. of F
Main Effects	36.183	7	5.169	.270	.965
Industry Type	36.183	7	5.169	.270	.965
Explained	36.183	7	5.169	.270	.965
Residual	12110.020	633	19.131		
Total	12146.203	640	18.978		

MANAGERIAL ASSISTANCE

Source of Variation	Sum of Squares	DF	Mean Square	F	Sig. of F
Main Effects	153.584	7	21.941	1.415	.196
Industry Type	153.584	7	21.941	1.415	.196
Explained	153.584	7	21.941	1.415	.196
Residual	10702.038	690	15.510		
Total	10855.622	697	15.575		

TECHNICAL ASSISTANCE

Source of Variation	Sum of Squares	DF	Mean Square	F	Sig. of F
Main Effects	140.043	7	20.006	1.060	.338
Industry Type	140.043	7	20.006	1.060	.338
Explained	140.043	7	20.006	1.060	.338
Residual	11986.520	635	18.876		
Total	12126.563	642	18.889		

CULTURAL INTERACTION

Source of Variation	Sum of Squares	DF	Mean Square	F	Sig. of F
Main Effects	134.318	7	19.188	1.773	.090
Industry Type	134.318	7	19.188	1.773	.090
Explained	134.318	7	19.188	1.773	.090
Residual	7303.173	675	10.820		
Total	7437.490	682	10.905		

INTERNALIZATION

Source of Variation	Sum of Squares	DF	Mean Square	F	Sig. of F
Main Effects	202.899	7	28.986	1.176	.314
Industry Type	202.899	7	28.986	1.176	.314
Explained	202.899	7	28.986	1.176	.314
Residual	16611.214	674	24.646		
Total	16814.113	681	24.690		

TABLE F9
ANALYSIS OF VARIANCE OF CRITERIA FOR EVALUATION
BY INDUSTRY GROUP (2-digit SIC)

TOTAL SALES DOLLARS

Source of Variation	Sum of Squares	DF	Mean Square	F	Sig. of F
Main Effects	40.853	7	5.836	1.886	.069
Industry Type	40.853	7	5.836	1.886	.069
Explained	40.853	7	5.836	1.886	.069
Residual	2141.391	692	3.094		
Total	2182.244	699	3.122		

NUMBER OF MBEs IN PROGRAM

Source of Variation	Sum of Squares	DF	Mean Square	F	Sig. of F
Main Effects	39.879	7	5.697	1.880	.070
Industry Type	39.879	7	5.697	1.880	.070
Explained	39.879	7	5.697	1.880	.070
Residual	2097.058	692	3.030		
Total	2136.937	699	3.057		

FEDERAL QUOTA

Source of Variation	Sum of Squares	DF	Mean Square	F	Sig. of F
Main Effects	105.498	7	15.071	4.724	.000
Industry Type	105.498	7	15.071	4.724	.000
Explained	105.498	7	15.071	4.724	.000
Residual	2198.017	689	3.190		
Total	2303.515	696	3.310		

HELPING AND DEVELOPING MBEs

Source of Variation	Sum of Squares	DF	Mean Square	F	Sig. of F
Main Effects	15.994	7	2.285	1.102	.360
Industry Type	15.994	7	2.285	1.102	.360
Explained	15.994	7	2.285	1.102	.360
Residual	1443.455	696	2.074		
Total	1459.449	703	2.076		

ESTABLISH PERSONAL RELATIONSHIPS

Source of Variation	Sum of Squares	DF	Mean Square	F	Sig. of F
Main Effects	63.283	7	9.040	2.914	.005
Industry Type	63.283	7	9.040	2.914	.005
Explained	63.283	7	9.040	2.914	.005
Residual	2150.069	693	3.103		
Total	2213.352	700	3.162		

TABLE F9 continued

CREATIVE USES OF MBEs

Source of Variation	Sum of Squares	DF	Mean Square	F	Sig. of F
Main Effects	13.557	7	1.937	1.016	.418
Industry Type	13.557	7	1.937	1.016	.418
Explained	13.557	7	1.937	1.016	.418
Residual	1326.421	696	1.906		
Total	1339.977	703	1.906		

INCREASING BUYERS' PORTFOLIOS

Source of Variation	Sum of Squares	DF	Mean Square	F	Sig. of F
Main Effects	7.996	7	1.142	.683	.687
Industry Type	7.996	7	1.142	.683	.687
Explained	7.996	7	1.142	.683	.687
Residual	1160.665	694	1.672		
Total	1168.661	701	1.667		

TABLE F10
ANALYSIS OF VARIANCE OF IMPEDIMENTS
BY JOB TITLE

SMALL NUMBERS

Source of Variation	Sum of Squares	DF	Mean Square	F	Sig. of F
Main Effects	946.194	3	315.398	5.559	.001
Job Title	946.194	3	315.398	5.559	.001
Explained	946.194	3	315.398	5.559	.001
Residual	33700.074	594	56.734		
Total	38913.916	692	58.034		

BUSINESS UNCERTAINTY

Source of Variation	Sum of Squares	DF	Mean Square	F	Sig. of F
Main Effects	25.622	3	8.541	.357	.784
Job Title	25.622	3	8.541	.357	.784
Explained	25.622	3	8.541	.357	.784
Residual	14067.811	588	23.925		
Total	14093.432	591	23.847		

PRODUCTION UNCERTAINTY

Source of Variation	Sum of Squares	DF	Mean Square	F	Sig. of F
Main Effects	70.046	3	23.349	1.055	.368
Job Title	70.046	3	23.349	1.055	.368
Explained	70.046	3	23.349	1.055	.368
Residual	12856.286	581	22.128		
Total	12926.332	584	22.134		

COMPLEXITY

Source of Variation	Sum of Squares	DF	Mean Square	F	Sig. of F
Main Effects	1528.938	3	509.646	2.311	.075
Job Title	1528.938	3	509.646	2.311	.075
Explained	1528.938	3	509.646	2.311	.075
Residual	126153.888	572	220.549		
Total	127682.826	575	222.057		

OPPORTUNISM

Source of Variation	Sum of Squares	DF	Mean Square	F	Sig. of F
Main Effects	78.240	3	26.080	1.272	.283
Job Title	78.240	3	26.080	1.272	.283
Explained	78.240	3	26.080	1.272	.283
Residual	11908.776	581	20.497		
Total	11987.015	584	20.526		

IMPACTED INFORMATION

Source of Variation	Sum of Squares	DF	Mean Square	F	Sig. of F
Main Effects	839.090	3	279.697	5.807	.001
Job Title	839.090	3	279.697	5.807	.001
Explained	839.090	3	279.697	5.807	.001
Residual	28126.480	584	48.162		
Total	28965.570	584	49.345		

ATMOSPHERE

Source of Variation	Sum of Squares	DF	Mean Square	F	Sig. of F
Main Effects	49.097	3	16.366	.349	.790
Job Title	49.097	3	16.366	.349	.790
Explained	49.097	3	16.366	.349	.790
Residual	27279.614	581	46.953		
Total	27328.711	584	46.796		

RESOURCE DEPENDENCE

Source of Variation	Sum of Squares	DF	Mean Square	F	Sig. of F
Main Effects	708.347	3	236.116	2.093	.100
Job Title	708.347	3	236.116	2.093	.100
Explained	708.347	3	236.116	2.093	.100
Residual	65667.307	582	112.830		
Total	66375.654	585	113.463		

TABLE F10 continued

VALUE SIMILARITY

Source of Variation	Sum of Squares	DF	Mean Square	F	Sig. of F
Main Effects	2345.031	3	781.677	4.214	.006
Job Title	2345.031	3	781.677	4.214	.006
Explained	2345.031	3	781.677	4.214	.006
Residual	108878.312	587	185.483		
Total	111223.343	590	188.514		

VALUE IMPORTANCE

Source of Variation	Sum of Squares	DF	Mean Square	F	Sig. of F
Main Effects	348.486	3	116.162	1.302	.273
Job Title	348.486	3	116.162	1.302	.273
Explained	348.486	3	116.162	1.302	.273
Residual	53080.693	595	89.211		
Total	53429.179	598	89.346		

TABLE F11
ANALYSIS OF VARIANCE OF ACTIVITY SCALES
BY JOB TITLE

MONITORING OF MBEs

Source of Variation	Sum of Squares	DF	Mean Square	F	Sig. of F
Main Effects	298.454	3	99.485	3.598	.013
Job Title	298.454	3	99.485	3.598	.013
Explained	298.454	3	99.485	3.598	.013
Residual	16397.389	593	27.652		
Total	16695.843	596	28.013		

MONITORING OF CORPORATIONS

Source of Variation	Sum of Squares	DF	Mean Square	F	Sig. of F
Main Effects	2112.169	3	704.056	6.268	.000
Job Title	2112.169	3	704.056	6.268	.000
Explained	2112.169	3	704.056	6.268	.000
Residual	65709.977	585	112.325		
Total	67822.146	588	115.344		

SEARCHING FOR MBEs

Source of Variation	Sum of Squares	DF	Mean Square	F	Sig. of F
Main Effects	619.163	3	206.388	7.823	.000
Job Title	619.163	3	206.388	7.823	.000
Explained	619.163	3	206.388	7.823	.000
Residual	15592.830	591	26.384		
Total	16211.993	594	27.293		

SEARCHING FOR CORPORATIONS

Source of Variation	Sum of Squares	DF	Mean Square	F	Sig. of F
Main Effects	1154.921	3	384.974	10.585	.000
Job Title	1154.921	3	384.974	10.585	.000
Explained	1154.921	3	384.974	10.585	.000
Residual	21203.423	583	36.370		
Total	22358.344	586	38.154		

FINANCIAL ASSISTANCE

Source of Variation	Sum of Squares	DF	Mean Square	F	Sig. of F
Main Effects	45.794	3	15.265	.778	.506
Job Title	45.794	3	15.265	.778	.506
Explained	45.794	3	15.265	.778	.506
Residual	10804.685	551	19.609		
Total	10850.479	554	19.586		

MANAGERIAL ASSISTANCE

Source of Variation	Sum of Squares	DF	Mean Square	F	Sig. of F
Main Effects	324.235	3	108.078	7.699	.000
Job Title	324.235	3	108.078	7.699	.000
Explained	324.235	3	108.078	7.699	.000
Residual	8310.409	592	14.038		
Total	8634.644	595	14.512		

TECHNICAL ASSISTANCE

Source of Variation	Sum of Squares	DF	Mean Square	F	Sig. of F
Main Effects	230.254	3	76.751	4.074	.007
Job Title	230.254	3	76.751	4.074	.007
Explained	230.254	3	76.751	4.074	.007
Residual	10306.254	547	18.842		
Total	10536.555	550	19.157		

CULTURAL INTERACTION

Source of Variation	Sum of Squares	DF	Mean Square	F	Sig. of F
Main Effects	159.459	3	53.153	4.897	.002
Job Title	159.459	3	53.153	4.897	.002
Explained	159.459	3	53.153	4.897	.002
Residual	6294.923	580	10.853		
Total	6454.382	583	11.071		

INTERNALIZATION

Source of Variation	Sum of Squares	DF	Mean Square	F	Sig. of F
Main Effects	325.263	3	108.421	4.426	.004
Job Title	325.263	3	108.421	4.426	.004
Explained	325.263	3	108.421	4.426	.004
Residual	14157.617	578	24.494		
Total	14482.880	581	24.928		

TABLE F12
ANALYSIS OF VARIANCE OF CRITERIA FOR EVALUATION
BY JOB TITLE

TOTAL SALES DOLLARS

Source of Variation	Sum of Squares	DF	Mean Square	F	Sig. of F
Main Effects	17.101	3	5.700	1.868	.134
Job Title	17.101	3	5.700	1.868	.134
Explained	17.101	3	5.799	1.868	.134
Residual	1815.223	595	3.051		
Total	1832.324	598	3.064		

NUMBER OF MBEs IN PROGRAM

Source of Variation	Sum of Squares	DF	Mean Square	F	Sig. of F
Main Effects	19.887	3	6.629	2.244	.082
Job Title	19.887	3	6.629	2.244	.082
Explained	19.887	3	6.629	2.244	.082
Residual	1757.429	595	2.954		
Total	1777.316	598	2.972		

FEDERAL QUOTA

Source of Variation	Sum of Squares	DF	Mean Square	F	Sig. of F
Main Effects	8.020	3	2.673	2.673	.474
Job Title	8.020	3	2.673	2.673	.474
Explained	8.020	3	2.673	2.673	.474
Residual	1896.272	593	3.198		
Total	1904.291	596	3.195		

HELPING AND DEVELOPING MBEs

Source of Variation	Sum of Squares	DF	Mean Square	F	Sig. of F
Main Effects	16.984	3	5.661	2.803	.039
Job Title	16.984	3	5.661	2.803	.039
Explained	16.984	3	5.661	2.803	.039
Residual	1207.667	598	2.020		
Total	1224.651	601	2.038		

ESTABLISH PERSONAL RELATIONSHIPS

Source of Variation	Sum of Squares	DF	Mean Square	F	Sig. of F
Main Effects	11.614	3	3.871	1.223	.301
Job Title	11.614	3	3.871	1.223	.301
Explained	11.614	3	3.871	1.223	.301
Residual	1890.608	597	3.167		
Total	1902.223	600	3.170		

CREATIVE USES OF MBEs

Source of Variation	Sum of Squares	DF	Mean Square	F	Sig. of F
Main Effects	15.768	3	5.256	2.795	.040
Job Title	15.768	3	5.256	2.795	.040
Explained	15.768	3	5.256	2.795	.040
Residual	1126.501	599	1.881		
Total	1142.269	602	1.897		

INCREASING BUYERS' PORTFOLIOS

Source of Variation	Sum of Squares	DF	Mean Square	F	Sig. of F
Main Effects	17.957	3	5.986	3.773	.011
Job Title	17.957	3	5.986	3.773	.011
Explained	17.957	3	5.986	3.773	.011
Residual	947.172	597	1.587		
Total	965.128	600	1.609		

THE CENTER FOR ADVANCED PURCHASING STUDIES •

THE CENTER FOR ADVANCED PURCHASING STUDIES (CAPS) was established in November 1986 as an affiliation agreement between the College of Business at Arizona State University and the National Association of Purchasing Management. It is located at The Arizona State University Research Park, 2055 East Centennial Circle, P.O. Box 22160, Tempe, Arizona 85285-2160 (Telephone [602] 752-2277).

The Center has three major goals to be accomplished through its research program:

- to improve purchasing effectiveness and efficiency;
- to improve overall purchasing capability;
- to increase the competitiveness of U.S. companies in a global economy.

Research under way and planned includes a Comparative Study of the Purchasing Process in the Manufacturing, Service, Retail/Trade/Distribution, and Government Sectors; Global Purchasing; World-Class Purchasing Organizations and Practices to 1995; Purchasing Roundtable; Purchasing Benchmarking; Impediments to Purchasing from Women-Owned Suppliers; Education and Training Requirements and Resources; and the Quality Issue.

CAPS, a 501 (c) (3) not-for-profit research organization, is funded solely by tax-deductible contributions from corporations and individuals who want to make a difference in the state of purchasing and materials management knowledge. Policy guidance is provided by the Board of Trustees consisting of:

The Center for Advanced Purchasing Studies and the National Association of Purchasing Management wish to thank the following corporations, foundations, individuals, and affiliated purchasing management associations for their financial support:

FIRMS

Americhem Inc.
Ameritech Services
ANR Freight System, Inc.
ARCO
ARGO-TECH Corporation
Avery, Materials Group
Barnes Group Foundation
The Bauer Group
BellSouth Services
BP America
Carter Chemicals & Services, Inc.

Caterpillar Inc.
Chevron U.S.A. Inc.
C.M. Almy & Sons, Inc.
Coastal Savings Bank
Concord Realstate Corp.
Corning Glass Works
CSX Transportation
Dragon Products Co.
DuPont/Conoco
Eastman Kodak Company
Ernst & Whinney

Exxon Company, U.S.A.
Firestone Trust Fund
Freeway Corp.
G.E. Company, Contracting/Purchasing
G.E. Company, Corporate Sourcing
The Glidden Company
Haluch & Associates
The HCA Foundation
Hughes Aircraft
Imperial Litho/Graphics, Inc.
Intel Corporation

International Minerals & Chemical
  Corporation
Keithley Instruments, Inc.
Kraft, Inc.
The Lincoln Electric Company
Lockheed Leadership Fund
Loctite Corporation
L-Tec Welding & Cutting Systems
Marathon Oil Company
Mobil Foundations, Inc.
North Canton Tool Company
Northern Telecom Inc.
NYNEX Materiel Enterprises Co.

Ohio Power Company
Olin Corporation Charitable
  Trust
OXY USA Inc.
Parker Hannifin Corporation
Polaroid Corporation
Raytheon Company
RJR Nabisco, Inc.
Shamrock Hose & Fitting
  Company
Shell Oil Company
Simmons Precision
  Product Inc.

Society Corporation
Southern Pacific Transportation Co.
Texaco Services, Inc.
Texas Instruments Incorporated
TRW Foundation
Union Camp Corporation
Union Pacific Railroad Co.
United Technologies Corporation
The Upjohn Company
U S WEST Business Resources, Inc.
Westinghouse Foundation

INDIVIDUALS

Diane K. Bishop
William A. Bales, C.P.M.
Robert Breitbart
Montague E. Cooper, C.P.M.
Frank Croyl
Walter Eads
Harold E. Fearon, Ph.D., C.P.M.
John H. Hoagland, Ph.D., C.P.M.
Robert L. Janson, C.P.M.

Robert Kaminski, C.P.M.
Dr. Kenneth H. Killen
Frederick W. Ludwig
Paul K. Moffat, C.P.M.
John P. Negrelli
R.D. Nelson
Robert P. Olson, C.P.M.
Harold F. Puff, Ph.D., C.P.M.
Jon E. Schmiedebusch

Stanley N. Sherman, Ph.D., C.P.M.
Jonathan R. Stegner
Arthur W. Todd
Robert F. Weber, Attorney at Law
Milton Welch
W.A. Westerbeck
Mr. & Mrs. Harry B. Wiggins

PURCHASING MANAGEMENT ASSOCIATIONS

Akron
Arkansas
Canton
Cinti Demetria
Cleveland
Colorado (Western)
Dallas
Dayton
Denver
Detroit
District VI
Florida Central
Florida First Coast
Florida Gold Coast
Florida Space Coast

Florida West Coast
Georgia
Iowa (Central)
Iowa (Eastern)
Kansas City
Lima
Madison Area
Maine
Maryland, Inc.
Michigan (Southwestern)
Michigan Assoc. (Western)
New Jersey
New Mexico
New Orleans, Inc.
Oklahoma City

Old Dominion, Inc. (Virginia)
Oregon
Northeastern PA
Petroleum Industry Buyers Group
Philadelphia, Inc.
Pittsburgh
Rhode Island
Spokane
Syracuse and Central New York, Inc.
Tennessee (East)
Toledo
Twin City
Washington (D.C.)
Youngstown District (Ohio)

CENTER FOR ADVANCED PURCHASING STUDIES
Arizona State University Research Park
2055 East Centennial Circle
P.O. Box 22160
Tempe, Arizona 85285-2160
(602) 752-2277

ISBN: 0-945968-03-5